May 68

The French Revolt

William Schnabel

FIRST EDITION

Library of Congress Cataloging–in–Publication Data
Schnabel, William.
    May 68: The French Revolt
    Includes index and bibliography
    1. May 68. 2. French history. 3. Radicalism. 4. Daniel Cohn-Bendit. 5. Police brutality 6. Charles de Gaulle

ISBN-13: 978-1984938688
ISBN-10: 1984938681

Book and cover design by Le Diable Ermite
Composition by Le Diable Ermite

Published by:
Le Diable Ermite
16 La Petite Rue
55140 Brixey-aux-Chanoines - France

10 9 8 7 6 5 4 3 2 1

Acknowledgements

I began thinking about this book with the approach of the fiftieth anniversary of May 1968. Youth today are, for the most part, unfamiliar with the French revolt that began at the University of Nanterre, so it seemed like a good idea to write something about this important social movement. I have attempted to give an honest and truthful account, knowing in advance that there is disagreement on some aspects of the revolt and strike, depending on one's political affiliation. For conservative Nicolas Sarkozy, "May 1968 forced moral and intellectual relativism on us." Daniel Cohn-Bendit, on the other hand, said "May 1968 engendered the ecology movement, women's liberation and anti-totalitarian sensibility."

I wish to thank the authors listed in the bibliography for the information they published on May 1968, notably Adrien Dansette, Jean-Pierre Le Goff, Laurent Joffrin, Jean-François Sirinelli, UNEF, SNE-sup, Maurice Grimaud, Christine Fauré, the National Audiovisual Institute, Jean-Luc Magneron, Daniel Cohn-Bendit and all the others. I also wish to thank Fabienne Dujet for her inspiration. Our animated conversations about "Dany le Rouge" and the barricades in Paris impelled me to go further.

Table of Contents

A Time to Revolt

Many French officials said they were taken by surprise when students demonstrated in Paris in May 1968, but the student reaction to the closing of the University of the Sorbonne was perfectly consistent with the Zeitgeist of the sixties and what was happening around the world. The sixties were a turbulent decade, with protests in the United States, Mexico, Brazil, Japan, Germany, Spain, Italy, Czechoslovakia, France and elsewhere. Much of the dissent was fueled by imperialism and the War in Vietnam, though certainly not all of it.

The Free Speech Movement on the U.C. Berkeley campus beginning on 1 October 1964, was one of the first important group protests on an American university campus. Some 2,000 students occupied Sproul Hall, the administration building, because they had been deprived of their First Amendment right of free speech. Though rebuked by university officials at the time, militants like Mario Savio, Jackie Goldberg and Jack Weinberg, who used civil disobedience to protest for rights, have become iconic heroes.

Columbia University in New York was the scene of a student strike which resulted in the occupation of campus buildings on 23 April 1968, lasting almost an entire week. Students demanded that the university stop collaborating with the Department of Defense, more specifically the Institute for Defense Analyses. Of course, that was something the university was not prepared to do, since it was a lucrative enterprise.

In Mexico, the assault on vocational schools during the third week of July resulted in demonstrations in July and August 1968, culminating in the infamous massacre in the Plaza de la Tres Culturas, during which about 400 students were shot to death by the police and the army.

Spanish students had long been fed up with Franco's totalitarian regime, and in April 1968 tens of thousands expressed their dissatisfaction openly. In Italy students demanded better working conditions on campus, as a result, Italian universities were occupied by students one after the other, beginning with Trente on 1 November 1967, followed by the Catholic University of Milan, and then the universities of Turin, Genoa, Pavia, Cagliari, Salerno, and Padua.

In Brazil, students began organizing protests against the military dictatorship in which generals assumed the post of president. 21 June 1968, became known as "Bloody Friday" when 28 people were killed during a march, 1,000 persons were arrested, and numerous police cars burned. The March of the One Hundred Thousand was a mass protest in Rio de Janeiro against the junta. To show they would not be intimidated despite the repression, some demonstrators carried a banner that read: "Down with the Dictatorship."

Japanese students, considered by some the best organized of the student protestors, occupied the University of Tokyo and Nihon University in June 1968, and designated their campuses as "liberated zones" where the police could not enter. Wearing yellow helmets and armed with long sticks, they freely engaged in combat with the police.

In West Germany, the assassination attempt against Rudi

Dutschke on 11 April 1968, one of SDS's most charismatic leaders, resulted in numerous demonstrations there and around the world.

There was a myriad of student protests in the sixties, and it would take several volumes to discuss them. The point here is simply to show that students were active and concerned about the world they were living in and were prepared to take the risk of defending their rights and opinions. In this sense May 68 in France was by no means an anomaly, but rather an episode in the international student movement.

It is no surprise that a great deal of the protest of the sixties was against the War in Vietnam, a war that was brought into the living rooms of Americans by television, forcing millions of average citizens to witness the horrors of U.S. military intervention in Southeast Asia, and thus militating against public indifference.

Vietnam had proclaimed its independence on 2 September 1945. Ho Chi Minh wrote the official declaration which was largely based on the American Declaration of Independence, proclaimed on 4 July 1776, in Philadelphia. In the beginning he believed the United States would help his country achieve freedom because the Americans had won their independence by rebelling against the English.

The United States military became involved in Indochina and Vietnam long before John F. Kennedy was elected the thirty-fifth president. President Dwight D. Eisenhower had sent American troops there, and the Office of Strategic Services (OSS), created in 1942, was very active in Indochina. Later, the Saigon Military Mission, created on 29 July 1954, by the CIA to wage war in Indochina, was the most powerful organization there between 1945 and 1975, according to John Newman, who describes its activities in *JFK and Vietnam*.

After the assassination of president Kennedy, who was planning on ending American involvement in Vietnam, Lyndon Johnson, whom Kennedy was going to discard as running mate in the upcoming election, had absolute control to escalate the war, which he did on an unprecedented scale. Congress gave him virtually unanimous support after the lie about the United States being attacked in the Gulf of Tonkin. The extent of U.S. involvement is made all too clear by the number of troops engaged in the war. In 1961 there were roughly 16,000 American advisers, technicians and soldiers in Vietnam; that number increased to 510,000 soldiers by December 1967 when Johnson was in the White House.

Protests against the war began with the teach-ins in the United States, the first of which was at the University of Michigan at Ann Arbor on 24 Mars 1965.

The March on the Pentagon was the major demonstration of 1967, occurring on 21 October. But there were many others. The National Student Association cited 221 significant demonstrations against the war on university campuses in the United States. The Youth International Party (Yippie) and the National Mobilization Committee to End the War in Vietnam (MOBE) went to Chicago in August 1968, during the Democratic National Convention, to protest the war.

In France, some of the first demonstrations were organized by the National Vietnam Committee (CVN) created in the fall of 1966 and led by Laurent Schwartz. Jean-Paul Sartre, Alfred Kastler and Vladimir Jankelevitch were members.

Leftist groups such as UNEF, FER, JCR, UJCML and the 22 March Movement were strongly opposed to imperialism and American intervention in Vietnam.

The massive marches for civil rights which began in the fifties and continued into the sixties were some of the most important protests of the decade. They were led by devoted leaders such as Martin Luther King and Medgar Evers. The Black protest movement became radicalized by the Black Panthers and the Student Nonviolent Coordinating Committee (SNCC) when their rights were not obtained, or were too slow in coming. These groups focused on the idea of Black Power, a term developed by Stokely Carmichael.

Militant Black leaders like Huey Newton, Bobby Seale, Stokely Carmichael and Malcom X changed the way many Blacks perceived themselves and advocated more radical means for achieving their goals, which is not to say that they were always successful. Their language and methods contrasted sharply with the nonviolent approach advocated by Nobel Prize winner Martin Luther King, but they all made it clear that civil rights and the right to protest for rights would continue to be an issue where racial discrimination existed.

May 68 began as a student movement. Many youths protesting in May and June 1968 in Paris were part of a counterculture, a term that was coined by Theodore Roszak, a history professor, in his book *The Making of the Counter Culture*. The counterculture, as its name suggests, was antithetical to mainstream, bourgeois culture, to the same extent that it rejected paternalism and authoritarianism, attitudes the radical baby-boomers associated with Charles de Gaulle and his government.

The counterculture, whose slogan was "total rejection," spurned virtually all aspects of modern society. The anti-university, founded in 1968 as a result of the Congress on the Dialectics of Liberation, an international symposium held in London's Roundhouse from 15 to 30 July 1967, exemplified this aspect of their ideology. It sought to "demystify human violence in all its forms and the social systems from which it emanates, and to explore new forms of action." Radical events at the University of Nanterre reiterated some of the notions of the anti-university.

Youths involved in the May movement wanted to be heard and needed a platform from which they could express their ideas. President Jean Roche of the University of the Sorbonne responded to conflicts with radical students by closing the university's doors and calling the police, which arrested students inside and outside the courtyard. This seemingly insignificant incident was the catalyst for the student revolt and related events of May 68. Frustration often leads to violence, and the lack of effective communication between opposing groups resulted in social disorder and bloodshed.

The Port Huron Statement–written in large part by Tom Hayden of Students for a Democratic Society, and published in 1962–says "apathy and alienation are products of our social institutions." Our social institutions then are the cause of many of our problems. Youths in the sixties criticized those institutions and sought change; not superficial change, for they wanted to revamp the structure of society with its inherent injustices and inequalities.

Students who were committed to the May 68 movement

were not "hippies," a derogatory term used by the media and the establishment to categorize young people with long hair that rejected their parents' values, the Puritan work ethic, capitalism, the American Dream, violence, imperialism, police state tactics, and so on. The psychedelic counterculture of the Haight-Ashbury of San Francisco, unlike the Berkeley radicals, was not politically militant, but the radical students from Nanterre and the Sorbonne said they were committed to bringing about change in an attempt to make society more egalitarian and more open, though many of their strategies were too shortsighted and limited in scope to be successful. As Jerry Rubin, Yippie and author of *Do It!* once said, there has to be something wrong with a society that causes so much agitation.

The Summer of Love ended on 6 October 1967, with the "Death of Hippie," a ritual ceremony to mark the end of a dream. In fact, the dream was over before that, though not everyone wanted to admit it. After "peace and love," watchword of the love generation, came the violence: the assassinations of Martin Luther King and Robert Kennedy, May 68, the Democratic National Convention and the police riots in Chicago, the Weathermen, *et al.* Despite peaceful protests the war continued to rage in Vietnam. Despite peaceful protests, Blacks continued to be discriminated against.

For the youth of May 1968, the real violence was the Cold War and the constant fear of annihilation that the older generation bequeathed to the children of the world. The real violence was dropping millions of tons of bombs, napalm and Agent Orange on a country seeking reunification by a leader heralded as the George Washington of his people. The real violence was the dehumanization of man by an economic system based on greed, waste and exploitation and a bureaucracy that cared more about statistics and numbers than real people. Those things were somewhere in the unconscious minds of the youths who revolted in Paris in May 1968.

Nanterre

The first events of May 68 began at the University of Nanterre, founded in 1964. Nanterre is a city to the west of Paris with a population of 90,332 in 1968. At the time of the French protests, Pierre Grappin, a German professor, was its president. There were about 11,000 students enrolled for the 1967-1968 school year, whereas today there are more than 33,000 and 2,000 professors, a dramatic change to say the least. Daniel Cohn-Bendit believed that the student movement in May 68 began at the University of Nanterre because it was new at the time and not yet under the influence of the unions or specific groups of students (DRE 127). As a result, the atmosphere was unlike that of the older universities in that innovative thinking and avant-garde ideas could be expressed more easily.

On 20 March 1968, during a heated demonstration organized by the National Vietnam Committee (CVN) for the victory of the Vietnamese people against American imperialism, dozens of youths, mostly students, invaded the American Express offices in Paris, at the corner of Auber and Scribe Streets, shouting "NLF will win," broke the pane glass window and burned an American flag. One of the radicals, Xavier Langlade, naive enough to go back to the scene of the crime to inspect the damage, was spotted by witnesses, arrested and taken to 36 Quai des Orfèvres where he was questioned by the police. That very night, four high school students were arrested at home. Nicolas Boulte, leader of the National Vietnam Committee, was arrested in the early morning. If the militants had only burned the American flag, probably not too much would have happened, but the urge to create an incident by destroying property was too great.

For Daniel Cohn-Bendit, this was a golden opportunity because Langlade was well-known at the University of Nanterre since he was associated with the Revolutionary Communist Youth (JCR) on campus, a Trotskyist association created by Alain Krivine in 1966.

A group of young radicals referred to as the Mad Dogs ("les enragés") made the rounds of the lecture halls to recruit as many students as they could for an assembly to protest "police brutality." At five o'clock p.m., about one hundred students were gathered in lecture hall B-2 to decide on a plan of action and discuss, among other things, the liberation of those who were arrested during the American Express incident.

The administrative tower on campus was chosen as the perfect building to occupy, especially since it was empty and there were only two caretakers present. The students immediately went to the top floor and set up camp in the faculty conference room, symbol of power. When the discussions were over and the beer cans were empty, it was decided to devote the 29th of March to debates about the organization of the university, the workers' struggle, the class war and anti-imperialism.

The way the 22 March Movement got its name says something about the group. Fidel Castro, the Cuban revolutionary and communist dictator, called his group the July 26 Movement because that was when the military barracks in Moncada were attacked. Daniel Cohn-Bendit and his friends named their revolutionary group the 22 March Movement in irony of the way the JCR idealized the Cuban revolution and Che Guevara. This improvised group of young zealots would play a key role in May 68 (JOF 49, SIR 63).

Pierre Grappin, university president, heard about the decision to use 29 March for revolutionary debates and quickly cancelled classes on Thursday and Friday in an effort to avoid further conflicts with radical students. Since there was no place else to go, the University of the Sorbonne in Paris was chosen.

Before describing the events at the Sorbonne, a brief glimpse at the preceding year can give an idea of how things evolved at the University of Nanterre.

On 29 March 1967, dozens of students had decided to invade the girls' dormitories on campus, something that was forbidden, and so president Grappin called the local police to have the male students removed. Many were shocked by this decision because traditionally the police were almost never used to solve university problems. This tradition dates back to the middle ages. In response to the president's decision, some two dozen male students, aided by the girls, occupied the dormitories for a week before obtaining permission to leave without having to reveal their identities, and without being punished by the university or the police.

But the university decided to pursue the matter, and a few days later twenty-nine students–twenty-five students that had occupied the dormitory plus four students who had not but were marked as "political militants"–received an official letter from the university informing them that they had broken the university's rules and had thus lost any right to have a room in a dormitory. The administration was careful to add, however, that the disciplinary sanctions were suspended.

One of the anecdotes often quoted with regards to May 1968, although not directly related to it, is Daniel Cohn-Bendit's swimming pool episode. François Missoffe, Minister of Sport and Youth, had gone to Nanterre to inaugurate a swimming pool on 8 January 1968. With a team of experts, he had previously written a long and rather tedious white paper on French youth. When one recalls the effervescence of the decade, the conclusion of his study is somewhat surprising. The paper affirmed that French youth dreamed of getting married early, that their main goal was to succeed in life, that politics was not a pressing issue for them, that there would not be a war, and that the future depended on the success of industry, domestic tranquility and the cohesiveness of the population.

Seeing an opportunity to deride the minister, Dany the Red approached him and with his predictable sarcasm said he had read the white paper on French youth, some six hundred pages of ineptitude, but not a single word was said about sexual problems. Missoffe, not to be nonplussed by the affront, sharply replied, "If you have those kinds of problems, you'd be advised to dive three times into the pool." Not to be outdone, Dany retorted, "That's exactly the kind of answer you'd get in a fascist regime" (JOF 68). To be fair to both sides, it must be admitted that there are several versions of the exchange, though apparently no recorded transcript exists.

Dany scored big with his fellow students that day and confirmed his growing notoriety of having the cheek to say what you want, to whoever you want, whenever you want. Needless to say, the university administration did not see things that way, and began discussing disciplinary action against him. In France, it is a crime to attack the honor and dignity of someone as stipulated in Article 29 of the Penal Code, the law of 1881 with regards to freedom of the press. But Dany was an agitator with a sharp tongue and a keen sense of repartee, who was prone to be sarcastic and verbally aggressive. He was born on 4 April 1945 in Montauban in the Tarn and Garonne department of France, but his parents were German. They had settled there after fleeing from the Nazis in 1933. Dany returned to Germany when he was thirteen, but he went back to France to enroll at the University of Nanterre, having been granted a German scholarship because he was an orphan.

Because of that incident the University of Nanterre decided to send him to another campus, taking advantage of the fact that his residence was in Paris, 2 Rue Léon-Giraud, in the nineteenth arrondissement, according to the General Intelligence Directorate.

Students accused the university of blacklisting rebels and dissidents and asking professors to prevent them from attending their courses: "At the end of the school year for 1967, a sociology professor received notice from university authorities telling him not to let such and such attend his classes, persons who would have been on the list of 29 [students], the famous blacklist" (DUT). In response to the accusations, the university printed an information circular on 29 January formally denying the existence of blacklists. One supposes that Daniel Cohn-Bendit would have been at the top of such a list if it existed. At the beginning of the university year, students learned that Daniel Cohn-Bendit was going to be transferred to a different university. Student reaction was predictable and immediate: a massive strike was organized in November 1967, in which ten to twelve thousand students participated, exchanging ideas on how best to deal with blacklists, corporatism and required class attendance.

When the strike was over, Daniel Cohn-Bendit was allowed to continue his studies in sociology at Nanterre, but shortly after he faced being deported since he was not French; he would acquire the French nationality much later, when he was seventy and no longer red but "green." Pierre Grappin had reportedly initiated, or helped to initiate, a procedure for deportation. An article mentions the affair in *Le Monde*, 28 January 1968. Daniel appeared before the deportation commission at the Paris police headquarters, defended by his attorney, François Sarda. In order to mitigate the harshness of his verbal joust with the French minister, he sent him a conciliatory letter, to which François Missoffe replied, inviting him to discuss some of the problems encountered by young people. As a result, the deportation procedure was annulled. Daniel Cohn-Bendit was learning a lot about power games, but what he probably did not know at the time was that the General Intelligence Directorate was keeping close tabs on him because of the Missoffe affair

(CHA).

The group of students that became known as the 22 March Movement was made up of a variety of ideologies: Christian leftists, Trotskyites, libertarians, Marxists, Maoists, Leninists, anarchists, antifascists, and so on. They seemed to be particularly interested in course content, the sexual taboos and neuroses of young people, but also American imperialism, particularly the War in Vietnam, and, of course, the economic structure of society. After the assassination attempt against Rudi Dutschke on 11 April 1968–a charismatic German radical who survived bullet wounds when he was shot by Joseph Backmann–a demonstration was organized down Saint Michel Boulevard in Paris on 12 April. A police van that drove by was bombarded with projectiles.

During the three or four years that preceded Mai 68, it was clear that the rift between the French Communist Party (PCF) and student radicals was growing ever wider, in fact, the PCF had become a prime target of radicals who felt the party and its paper, *L'Humanité*, were soft on American imperialism (SIR 65).

This helps to explain why, for example, Pierre Juquin, communist representative and central committee member of the PCF, was booed and forced to flee radicals at Nanterre on 26 April 1968, and why Georges Marchais attacked student radicals in an article in *L'Humanité* published on 3 May 1968, calling them children of the bourgeoisie that played into the hands of capitalist monopolies, and fake revolutionaries that needed to be unmasked.

On Saturday, 27 April, Daniel Cohn-Bendit was arrested while leaving his apartment at 8 a.m., in part because of a tract circulating at Nanterre signed "22 March": on the last page were instructions on how to make Molotov cocktails (JOF 77). To complicate things for Dany, Yves Kervendaël was wounded in a brawl in front of the National Federation of French Students (FNEF), a conservative organization. Kervendaël lodged a formal complaint and mentioned Cohn-Bendit. Because of the complaint, the police could question Dany, which they did for almost twelve hours. Maurice Grimaud, the prefect in Paris, says in his book they did not want to create a martyr, and felt that the university should handle its own problems, though he was not opposed to "reproving the popular agitator" (GRI 76). Dany was released before 8 p.m.

An exposition to honor South Vietnamese soldiers who were victims of communist aggression was organized on Sunday, 28 April, at 44 Rue de Rennes, by Roger Holeindre, a rightwing militant. Suddenly, a Renault 4 came to an abrupt stop, weapons were taken out of the car, and the passengers entered the building with another group that had been waiting in the street. The exposition was ransacked and the militant leftists got in a brawl with the skinheads inside. UJCML later claimed responsibility for the attack, saying they could not stand to see "fascists" organizing an exhibition in favor of South Vietnam (JOF 78).

2 May was the first day of the anti-imperialist days at Nanterre, organized by the 22 March Movement. The group had requested a classroom for their various workshops. Since the administration was thought to be dragging its heels, Dany and friends invaded their offices to make their demands more urgent. The administration conceded but the radicals

thought the room was not capacious enough, so they occupied René Rémond's lecture hall and taped a scribbled note on the door: "Rémond's class is canceled." When the professor entered with his students, somebody threw a bench at him, so he left.

After the destruction of the rightwing exhibition the previous Sunday, rumors were circulating about Occident looking for revenge—fear of reprisals by the dreaded extremists was widespread that day.

Occident was founded in April 1964. From 1965 to 1968, there were probably about 800 to 1,000 members. It was impossible to know the exact number because that information was kept secret. The group was anti-liberal because liberalism was believed to be the enemy of nationalism. Fascism was seen as a positive political movement that could bring the nation's young people to power. Occident's propaganda was anticommunist, and the organization supported the dictators in South Vietnam and American involvement there. The group's name was indicative of its goal to defend the West against the East and the Soviet bloc during the Cold War. In the Latin Quarter of Paris the group used violence against leftwing militants, La Joie de lire bookstore, and the café Champollion. During May 1968, the group was responsible for numerous provocations against radicals, and an undeclared war was going on between the two groups. On 31 October 1968, Raymond Marcellin, Minister of the Interior, banned Occident.

Added to the seething atmosphere at Nanterre was the fact that eight 22 March students, including Cohn-Bendit, Duteuil and Castro, had received notice to appear before the disciplinary council of the university on 6 May (JOF 83).

Fearing renewed violence on campus, president Grappin closed the University and cancelled all classes.

3 May

For all practical purposes, May 68 began on 3 May 1968 at the University of the Sorbonne, 1 Rue Cousin. Since the University of Nanterre was closed, the 22 March Movement transferred its meeting to Paris and the Sorbonne.

The assembly in the courtyard of the Sorbonne was essentially a protest meeting: protest against the closure of Nanterre, but also support for the eight militants to be brought before the disciplinary council. Like most protest meetings, it involved a minority of Paris students, maybe 0.4% of all the students (BAY 23), based on the fact that there were an estimated four hundred spectators present, half of whom were from Nanterre. Some militants were wearing helmets and were armed with shields and clubs (DAN 90).

The speakers addressed the crowd from the steps of the chapel. The meeting was predictable and, for the most part, unexciting, since it involved the usual dose of militant clichés. Henri Weber spoke for the JCR, de Bresson for FER, Jacques Sauvageot for UNEF, Daniel Cohn-Bendit for 22 March. His rhetoric was thought to be more unusual than most because "He knows how to say out loud in simple terms what nobody dares to confusedly think" (BAY 24). At 1 p.m. students were more than eager to take a break for lunch at the university restaurant for students, familiarly called "resto U," large cafeterias that serve complete meals to students at very cheap prices.

The meeting resumed at 2 p.m. and the crowd had swelled with students from the Unified Socialist Party (PSU), Union of Communist Students, and an unidentified group from Nanterre in busses reportedly filled with cobblestones.

At 3 p.m. a procession of Occident militants was coming from the Observatory. It was channeled by the police on Saint-Michel Boulevard and directed towards Maubert Square.

A rumor was being spread that "the Occident fascists [were] going to attack the meeting," the "fafs" (fascists) were gathering at the end of Saint-Michel Boulevard. The extremist nationalists had earlier distributed a tract entitled "Everyone United against the Riffraff." Occident was determined to "crush the Bolshevik vermin." It declared it had no intention of letting the pro-Chinese and anarcho-Trotskyists transform Paris into Berlin. The day before a fire was started in the premises of the humanities study group (FGEL), a group connected to UNEF.

An eerie feeling of panic was taking hold of the assembly. JCR and UJCML decided to use their security forces in the Sorbonne to protect the faculty and the campus [sic], when in truth, Occident was not planning on attacking at all. Maybe the paranoia and pavid reactions were just part of a desire, conscious or unconscious, to be in the spotlight, to appear to be important. Because the radicals feared an imminent attack, some reportedly started breaking tables and chairs in an area in front of the lecture halls to make weapons. At least that is Alain Peyrefitte's version. UNEF denies the minister's claims by saying the pieces of wood came from an old broken table lying in a corner of the courtyard (LN 12). Some students were gathering rocks from a nearby construction site. The "security" for the different groups was posted at the entrances and exits, looking as though they would kill anyone not belonging to the right organization. While this was going on, classes were being conducted on all levels. Faculty members did not know what was happening, but it looked dangerous.

At three o'clock the university decided to close the doors to the amphitheaters and classrooms. At four o'clock Jean Roche, head of the university, cancelled classes and asked students to evacuate the campus (BAY 26). As expected, militants in the courtyard refused to leave. Jean Roche tried to contact the Minister of Education and the Paris prefect. During a conversation with Alain Peyrefitte's cabinet, he was told that the situation called for police intervention. He asked the head of the cabinet to send the police to avoid a brawl between radicals and rightwing extremists. The ministry was reticent to do so because Peyrefitte was opposed to police intervention on university campuses (DAN 90). The day before, Maurice Grimaud sent a detailed report to the Minister of the Interior in which he expressed his opposition to police intervention in university affairs. This probably explains why the authorities at police headquarters requested a written request.

At 15:35 p.m. the police chief at the fifth arrondissement station received an explosive message: "The rector of the academy of Paris […] requires police assistance to re-establish order in the interior of the Sorbonne by expelling the troublemakers" (CHA).

This message shows that Roche wanted the police to get rid of the students at the radical meeting and not to prevent Occident from going on campus. He believed the radicals were capable of disrupting normal university activities such as classes and examinations. Roche was particularly concerned about the "agrégation" examination that was scheduled to begin the following Monday.

The police intervened at 4:40 p.m. to forcibly remove the people attending the meeting. They came on campus by the Rue des Écoles and expelled the students by the Rue de la Sorbonne. Technically, the students were not arrested, though they were loaded like cattle into police vans and taken to different locations to verify their identities. Maurice Grimaud, prefect of Paris, said things were going quietly until a police captain decided to check identification at police headquarters and not at the Sorbonne, adding that this decision was not sufficiently thought out because it was routine procedure to do so (GRI 15, 18). Routine or not, that decision was the spark that ignited the tinderbox.

Daniel Cohn-Bendit and Jacques Sauvageot were among the students loaded into the paddy wagons. Students had gathered around the police vehicles in the Latin Quarter and were chanting: "Free our comrades," "CRS-SS" (though in fact the units involved were not CRS), or "Stop the repression."

The first convoy of paddy wagons (three vans) managed to leave without too much difficulty at 5:10 pm. The problems started with the second convoy at 5:15 p.m. There was pushing and shoving around the vehicles and a van's tire had been deflated, so passengers had to be moved from one van to another. At 5:16 p.m. one thousand demonstrators arrived from Rue Champollion, moving towards the Sorbonne. Police reports said they were stupefied by the student violence and used teargas to clear the area. Some of the prisoners from one of the vans managed to escape.

In the eyes of the students, the police were clearly the aggressors, and as such the students had a legitimate right to defend their comrades. Students showed they were capable of mobilizing large numbers to protect not only themselves, but their ideas as well. Those who were not taken into custody, because there were not enough police vehicles, reacted immediately: barricades were erected with cobblestones and police became the target of stones and other projectiles; a police assistance van was attacked and one of the occupants was seriously injured when a stone crushed his face. According to Jacques Baynac, it was a young taxi driver who calmly walked up the street and heaved the cobblestone through the windshield, seriously injuring Christian Brunet, the policeman sitting on the right-hand side of the front seat (BAY 32). He would be in a coma for twelve days. A photographer took several shots of the incident on Friday, 3 May 1968, at 5:30 p.m. The license plate number of the police van was clearly visible: 5361 AB 75. The young man who threw the heavy stone did not look like a taxi driver. There was traffic in the street and the man was acting alone.

Many have wondered what would have happened if the students had not been detained. If they had not been transferred to the police stations, there would not have been any reasonable motivation to confront the Paris authorities, so it seems likely there would not have been the violence that occurred that day in the Latin Quarter. Police reports said tear-gas was widely used. In light of the film documentaries that exist for that day, this was an understatement.

For a long time, it seems the dialogue, if it can be called that, between young people and the older generation had been one of a parent to a child, not one between two adults. The condescending tone of that form of communication was no longer accepted by many youths in 1968. Police vans were "furiously attacked by the comrades of the students that the police had arrested to take to Beaujon" (GRI 83). In Grimaud's words, there was a riot in the street outside of the Sorbonne. In all there were 574 arrests, of which 179 were minors, 45 women, and 58 foreigners. Beaujon, the infamous "identification center," was described by those who were sent there as a kind of gulag or concentration camp, with barbed wire encircling the interior courtyard. It was not equipped to detain hundreds of people.

Grimaud gave orders to release the young girls and minors, the rest were released at two in the morning (GRI 83-84). How the police expected them to get home is not said. Twenty-seven were kept longer because of reported acts of violence and the illegal possession of weapons used for hand-to-hand combat. He was not referring to guns.

The General Intelligence Directorate took special care to keep the 574 files of the persons taken into custody on 3 May 1968 (CHA). Reading them today is both enlightening and slightly amusing, when one considers how they evolved. The outspoken leaders were all picked up of course: Alain Krivine (JCR), who later became a representative for Workers' Struggle and the Revolutionary Communist League;

Jacques Sauvageot (UNEF), who would become director of the École des beaux arts in Rennes; and the ever present Daniel Cohn-Bendit, who would become co-president of the Greens-European Free Alliance, and a representative at the European Parliament. There was also Brice Lalonde, who would become Minister of the Environment, a Green Party leader, and ambassador for negotiations with regards to global warming; and also José Rossi, future Minister of Industry in the government of Edouard Balladur, and president of the Corsican Assembly. Journalists who were arrested included: Guy Hocquenghem; Hervé Chabalier, future founder of the Capa agency; and Bernard Guetta, future director of the *Nouvel Observateur*, and journalist for France Inter.

Christian Fouchet, Minister of the Interior from 6 April 1967 to 31 May 1968, wanted to know what was going to be done with the ringleaders: Cohn-Bendit, Jacques Sauvageot, and Pierre Rousset (one of the JCR leaders). Of course Cohn-Bendit had not been arrested for violent acts, but for being at the Sorbonne, so any disciplinary action against him was the responsibility of the university and not the responsibility of the police. Paul Pageaud, public prosecutor, would decide what to do with the leaders. He was in favor of prosecuting only the obvious cases of violence. Louis Joxe, on the other hand, the Minister of Justice, said he was thoroughly shocked by the events in the Latin Quarter and wanted to prosecute all twenty-seven arrestees and keep Cohn-Bendit in police custody, to keep him out of mischief. Maurice Grimaud responded by saying it would be a mistake to hold the leader of 22 March because he could use it as an alibi for not appearing before the disciplinary council of the Sorbonne. As for prosecuting all the arrestees, Grimaud reiterated what the public prosecutor had said. Louis Joxe quickly sent his "instructions," which probably came from the Élysée Palace, to the public prosecutor's office. They undoubtedly played a role in the court's ruling.

On Saturday and Sunday, thirteen students went before the magistrate: one was acquitted and eight were given suspended sentences on Saturday; but four were sentenced to two months in prison on Sunday. The verdict was intended to set an example, though it would infuriate thousands of students who interpreted it as just another example of establishment hypocrisy and the double standard of the judicial system. It was highly unusual for the courts to convene on Sunday, and clearly demonstrated the government's desire to act quickly.

Daniel Cohn-Bendit and his comrades were scheduled to present their case at the Sorbonne on Monday, 6 May. Georges Pompidou, on an official trip to Iran and Afghanistan, was absent from France. Although the Prime Minister was adamant about not letting irresponsible students destroy French universities–Pompidou had the highest marks at the "agrégation" examination in French literature–he rejected the idea of deporting the German student.

6-7 May

Daniel Cohn-Bendit and the Mad Dogs could not have been happier with the results of the radical meeting at the Sorbonne on Friday, 3 May. It greatly accelerated their revolutionary movement and produced more tangible results than several months of harassing the university administration at Nanterre could have.

The National Union of Higher Education (SNE-sup) declared its solidarity with the students and called for a general strike in all French universities. If followed, it could have enormous consequences, and not just on the campuses.

SNE-sup representatives assembled at the École Normale supérieure in Rue d'Ulm with, for the first time, leaders of various student organizations: UNEF, PSU, JCR, FER, UJCML, 22 March Movement. These groups comprised the task force that would often meet to evaluate the changing situation and make strategic decisions. Soon they would be joined by High School Student Committees of Action (CAL). The Union of Communist Students (UEC) was absent because the French Communist Party (PCF) had rejected these leftwing groups. Obliquely referring to them, Georges Marchais spoke of small groups that "did not represent anything" (DAN 92).

Two demonstrations were planned for Monday, 6 May. One was scheduled for 9 a.m. to support Daniel Cohn-Bendit, the other at 6:30 p.m. to protest the condemnations of the protestors. At about the same time, UNEF was deprived of its government subsidy for the year. This decision was probably a consequence of its involvement in the radical movement, and made it difficult for the student union to function.

Cohn-Bendit and the other revolutionaries were in good company at the Sorbonne. Paul Ricœur, Henri Lefebvre and Alain Touraine marched alongside the defendants who sang the *Internationale:* "C'est la lutte finale / Groupons nous et demain / L'Internationale / sera le genre humain." Normally, disciplinary procedure required the accused to appear before the council individually, but the defendants demanded to be judged as a group. The hearing lasted four hours. Outside, Dany said they had enjoyed themselves immensely for four hours.

In the street, a boisterous throng of three thousand students had come to support their comrades (JOF 96). The Movement for University Action (MAU) called for the creation of committees capable of expanding the Movement to different universities, and why not in the workplace? Vietnam committees were cited as an example. Action committees were also being set up in local high schools with success. Maurice Najman and Michel Récanti were two such organizers.

The crowd of supporters was forced to disperse during the audience of the accused. This it did begrudgingly after the first teargas grenades and the first cobblestones were thrown. From the beginning it seemed that many demonstrators were itching for a fight; some were wearing helmets and were armed with sticks and metal bars. Human chains sprang up spontaneously, passing cobblestones to demonstrators who could throw the best. Many noticed that the efforts of the demonstrators were well-organized and well-synchronized.

At around six o'clock p.m. the riot ended, since the demonstrators were needed for the march scheduled to begin at Denfert-Rochereau Square. Police were forced to retreat from their position because they were getting crossfire from the Rue du Four. Apparently, this was the first time that the police had to yield ground to demonstrators.

The images of the riot were apocalyptic. The sounds, the sights and the smells were those of a civil war, or something close to it. Screams and angry threats pierced the fog of the teargas as silhouettes ran in and out of the burning mist that scorched people's lungs and eyes. Intermittent explosions made people jump nervously. Innocent bystanders were viciously clubbed for simply being in the wrong place at the wrong time, and raging fires cast an eerie specter in the hellish night, their flames devouring an overturned automobile that agonized on its side. A ghost truck in flames roared towards a police roadblock and smashed into a building. The manic desire to hurt had seized the passions of many and civilization retreated into empty spaces to lick its wounds.

Two huge pumper trucks with fire hoses arrived to dampen the spirits of the rioters and were showered in a hail of rocks; somebody heaved a cobblestone that smashed through the windshield, forcing the trucks to retreat from the front lines. Dozens of CRS charged the protestors, blindly swinging their sticks in the air, only to be submerged in a tempest of bottles, Molotov cocktails and unidentifiable projectiles. A grenadier was running blindly until he smacked right into a tree and fell dazed to the ground. Police were unable to launch another attack because of the violence of the crowd. Changing tactics, they managed to dislodge the demonstrators from the rear, and so the crowd flowed like a torrent into the Rue de Rennes. It was past 9 p.m. before the forces of law and order controlled the neighborhood. From then on it was merely a question of pursuing small groups of protestors and beating them to a pulp when they were caught.

The next morning the street was unrecognizable. It looked like a war zone, with the pavement torn up, cobblestones strewn everywhere, windows broken, the gutted carcasses of automobiles in the middle of the street, and the acrid smell of teargas that still poisoned the air.

Alain Peyrefitte, forty-two years old at the time, went on television in the evening, interviewed by Yves Mourousi. His demeanor contrasted sharply with the events of the preceding night. He was calm, rational and seemed sincere. "The forces of law and order entered the Sorbonne because the forces of disorder had entered the university," he said. There were three hundred students at a radical meeting of which one hundred were armed, those who were not broke up tables and chairs to use the legs of the furniture for weapons. A rightwing group tried to get on campus. He also said that some of the violence was caused by people who were not students, and who had no business being on campus. Jean Roche was naturally alarmed by the situation, so he asked for police assistance. That was his explanation.

With regards to the *riots*, a word never uttered by the Minister of Education, he said the demonstrations were deplorable, but less violent than demonstrations in Berlin, Warsaw, Bonn, Rome, Algiers, and the University of Columbia in New York.

When questioned about his "minimizing" the violence, Peyrefitte replied that the demonstration was serious, and rejected the claim that he was minimizing the gravity of the situation. There were 605,000 students in France and 160,000 students in Paris. The vast majority wanted to be allowed to study peacefully. The forces of law and order only intervened to protect those who wanted to study in peace.

When asked what Georges Pompidou's government was

going to do, his response was: "We say 'yes' to constructive dialogue and 'no' to violence. We must stop the escalation of violence and calm things down. Everyone must be allowed to reflect calmly. Paris was not chosen for the peace negotiations between the United States and North Vietnam because radicals from Nanterre demonstrate. Paris was chosen because it is a peaceful capital. Those that commit violent acts will see that violence turns against them. Calm must be restored. Examinations must take place and classes held again in the next few days at the Universities of Nanterre and the Sorbonne. That is what we wish to see happen."

Alain Peyrefitte was asked whether he sympathized with young people, meaning students, or with the older generation. The government, he said, was not an instrument whose goal was to divide teachers and students. It served the interests of the nation. It wanted the national interests to be respected. It was in the nation's interests for its universities to function peacefully. It was also in the nation's interests for its universities to be modernized, to be open to society and society to be open to its institutions of higher education. Everyone must collaborate to achieve that goal.

Despite the minister's plea for calm, a ritualistic pattern of violence was developing between youth and police, between two generations who no longer understood each other, who probably *never* understood each other. They were locked in a dangerous game–a game of defiance, revolt and uproar. For the time being, public opinion was sympathetic towards the students, but that could change.

The government, for its part, needed to explore ways for greater synergy between ministries, as perception of the student crisis varied considerably from one bureau to the next. For Charles de Gaulle, this was really nothing new for the Latin Quarter. He tried to shrug it off when he said: "It's not a serious peripeteia. The State must be respected and must make sure it is respected. We needed to be implacable to quell violence in the street. We needed to arrest 500 students every evening" (DAN 107). Those remarks aside, he did believe that the problem should be solved by his ministers. After all, that was their job. The government certainly did not want the violence to escalate, and, most importantly, it did not want to see anyone killed. But it was clear to everyone that it did not have control of the situation and that attitudes were becoming polarized.

On the morning of 7 May, Alain Peyrefitte met with James Marangé, head of the Federation of National Education (FEN), and Jean Daubard, head of the National Union of Primary School Teachers. They felt the minister was open to suggestions, though they seriously doubted whether the militant leftists could get their troops to obey. And there were many youths who were not students, who were loyal to no one, and simply hell-bent on creating mayhem.

During the Council of Ministers, the primary concern was for the classes and the examinations. Charles de Gaulle was quoted there as saying: "A riot is like a fire–you have to fight it in the first few minutes."

Jacques Sauvageot did not care much for the summary of the Council and even called it a "provocation" because the three student demands were not mentioned. Alain Geismar said the students would be in control of the Sorbonne, which had become the emblem of the student revolt in May.

Alain Peyrefitte, though eager to reopen Nanterre and the Sorbonne, insisted that it be reopened under "normal conditions." "If order is reestablished, everything is possible; if order is not reestablished, nothing is possible" (DAN 108). Alain Geismar and Jacques Sauvageot seemed to be favorable, but there were radical groups not prepared to give reassurance.

More than 6,000 students showed up for the demonstration beginning at 6:30 p.m. starting at Denfert-Rochereau. The pre-established itinerary was followed: Saint-Germain Boulevard, Rue de Seine, Rue de Tournon, Rue de Médicis, Edmond-Rostand Square. The police had set up a solid roadblock on Saint-Michel Boulevard to prevent marchers from heading towards the Sorbonne, which was still closed. Maurice Grimaud warned them not to try to get by the barrier when he saw a group moving in that direction. Dispersion at the conclusion of the march was orderly. There was no riot. Things were generally quieter when it rained, and it rained cats and dogs.

8 May

A fragile calm reigned on 8 May. There was no new fighting. Opposition to the government was rising and seemed absolute if you spoke to certain radical groups. It was clearly no longer simply a question of having one's demands met; it was about defiance, rejection and territoriality, which is to say communicating ownership or occupancy of specific areas. The violence with which the students reacted to the arrival of the police at the Sorbonne and the subsequent closing and desire to reoccupy the university seemed to reveal deeper aspects of human relations, such as territorial imperative, an emotion that human beings have maintained since the dawn of man. Student intransigence underscored this fact: "We won't move until they've given us back the Sorbonne" (DAN 118).

MAU, JCR and 22 March said the Movement had to remain intransigent to maintain its dynamic, its energy. In short, play the psychological game of confrontation and escalation. Once public opinion had been polarized, the students could take advantage of the situation. What this boiled down to was that many radical groups were firmly opposed to compromise (JOF 114). But confrontation and escalation, like all psychological games, is destructive, like playing with hand grenades or Molotov cocktails. And the destruction could go either way.

On the other hand, SNE-sup, UNEF, FER and the Troskyists seemed inclined to negotiate. Guerilla street fighting was not their objective. Unions usually seek to see their demands satisfied. Workers' unions, such as the FEN and CGT, were more inclined to seek a compromise, usually for their own interests. Once students began a social movement, workers' unions liked to take over and control it for their own purposes. The CGT was often accused of this by students.

For the time being, UNEF was anxious to maintain its privileged position in the student movement, so it organized an assembly at the faculty of science. Alain Geismar and Jacques Sauvageot got permission from Dean Marc Zamansky, mathematician, to use the large courtyard of Jussieu, formerly the Halle aux vins, for their meeting at six o'clock. In turn, police organized a strategic plan of action around the Sorbonne and Saint-Michel Boulevard in anticipation of any outbreaks of violence. They were reassured when it started to rain.

At seven o'clock, about 7,000 students had assembled (GRI 139). The principle leaders of the movement were there: Cohn-Bendit, Geismar, Sauvageot. Alfred Kastler and Jacques Monod, winners of the Nobel Prize, were also on hand, not preaching violence, of course. Movement leaders wanted to end the evening on a positive note, so they contacted the police there to see if they could march to the Latin Quarter. They agreed to conduct their march in an orderly manner and to disperse upon arrival. Maurice Grimaud said he was anxious to see if UNEF security could do its job and did not feel there was much of a risk, so he gave his approval.

While at the National Assembly, Alain Peyrefitte responded to a question from the opposition by saying that if certain conditions were met, classes could resume at the Sorbonne as soon as the president and the deans thought it was possible, which Peyrefitte hoped would be in the afternoon of the next day. A reporter from *France Soir* heard that and jumped the gun, thinking the crisis was resolved (JOF 115). The paper optimistically came out with a special edition announcing the resumption of classes as a sure thing. The newspaper *Combat* came out the next day with encouraging headlines for students as well: "De Gaulle Yields." Because of the press, militants began thinking they were about to win. Maurice Grimaud wanted to feel optimistic, too, since he had fewer CRS at his command as a result of the demonstrations in western France.

At seven o'clock about 7,000 students assembled on the campus of Jussieu: a vast marketplace where wine was once sold. The atmosphere at the Halle aux vins that evening was somewhat ambiguous. The PCF, that had distanced itself from the radical movement, in part because of the violence, sent its representatives to sniff around and see what was going on, denounce the provocateurs and plead for calm.

Dany the Red was late, busy answering questions for the BBC, but he soon noticed the change in atmosphere. "It was bound to happen," someone said, "the organizations have sold out again." Later, in a discussion with members of SNE-sup, Alain Geismar argued, "Don't you see that our action doesn't correspond at all with the logic of the Movement. . . . By promoting unity between the unions we have shackled the Movement, which is exactly the opposite of what most of us want. We've fallen into the political trap of the liberals and the conservatives. As a result we have to abandon people who are not students, who are proof that the Movement was beginning to get out of its ghetto" (JOF 118). What also disturbed Geismar was the fact that the police had freed French students that were in custody, but did not free foreigners or workers.

Slowly but surely, unions were taking over the Move-

43

ment. Yet it had all been started by students. The next day, militant leaders felt the same way, so, to try and get it back, they added a fourth demand. The student demands were: 1) open the Sorbonne, 2) evacuate the police from the Latin Quarter, 3) free all students imprisoned during the demonstrations, and 4) Maurice Grimaud, the prefect, the person they saw as responsible for the violence, must be replaced. It is unsure if this last demand was made public.

9 May

The student movement had reached its zenith of popularity. A poll conducted by the French Institute of Public Opinion (IFOP) the day before in Paris found that 61% of the persons polled said they were in favor of the student movement, and only 16% found the three student demands unjustified, or one Parisian in six.

Student militants, led by Daniel Cohn-Bendit, voted for the continuation of the Movement and decided to demonstrate on Friday evening at 6:30 p.m.

Georges Séguy of the CGT and Jacques Sauvageot of the UNEF met to discuss future strategy and the possibility of an expansion of the Movement. Séguy, who was deported by the Gestapo in Toulouse when he was seventeen, was appalled by the loudmouth, know-it-all attitude of Sauvageot. To begin with, UNEF was an hour late for the meeting. Séguy's description is worth mentioning: "We were invited to go inside the central headquarters, and the place was a pigsty: a table buried in papers, broken chairs, ashtrays overflowing with cigarette butts, empty bottles, half-eaten sandwiches, bandages and hardhats strewn everywhere" (SEG 19). The person in charge finally arrived, but it was an unkempt, unshaven Alain Geismar. Séguy pointed out that he had come to talk things over with UNEF, not with SNE-sup, upon which Geismar withdrew. Sauvageot arrived a little later.

Needless to say, this left a bad impression on the General Secretary of the CGT. Union members were punctual, well-groomed and usually respectful. The CGT found UNEF's radical slogans way too offensive for respectable people. No agreement was reached between the two antagonistic unions, and the CGT would be mistrustful of the radicals from thereon out.

General de Gaulle flew off the handle when he saw the front page of *Combat* and the headline: "De Gaulle gives in." University president Jean Roche, however, announced that classes would be held, and that Cohn-Bendit's disciplinary procedure had been deferred *sine die*.

At about two in the afternoon the French poet and novelist Louis Aragon was in the crowd of some two thousand young people who were still locked out of the Sorbonne. Alain Geismar offered a *mea culpa* by admitting his mistake in saying students would soon be sleeping in the Sorbonne, and Jacques Sauvageot, who always found something to say, promised it would be occupied as soon as it was reopened, as did the University Action Movement (MAU). Police informants in the crowd were carefully taking note of everything.

Aragon, adulated by some, hated by others, was signing autographs when a group yelled out in derision: "Vive the Guépéou! Vive Staline!" The provocations were not appreciated by everyone. Dany the Red was trying to figure out what all the hubbub was about. After he realized it was because of Aragon, he immediately yelled out his name and offered him the megaphone. When the crowd saw that it was Louis Aragon, they spurned him by catcalling to prevent him from talking. "This is not Krondstadt. Everyone has the right to talk, here, however much he is a traitor," quipped Dany. According to Jacques Baynac, nobody was better at denouncing Spanish militants opposed to Stalin residing in France (BAY 71). Cut short by the aggressive, hostile atmosphere of the crowd, the poet promised to gather as many allies as possible and to devote the next issue of *Les Lettres françaises* to the student revolt, then exited amidst derision mixed with adulatory applause. Those who read *L'Humanité* the next day could not help but notice that for the first time the baby-boomer "revolutionaries" were not insulted.

Pro-Chinese militants spoke next and proposed the slogan "the Sorbonne for the CRS." They wanted to turn it into a caserne. The only thing that could save the bourgeois movement headed by Dany the Red and others was an alliance with the working class. The undercurrent in the radical factions was making it more and more difficult to know when they were being serious and when they were wisecracking. And discord among the factions was so palpable that day you could cut it with a knife. UJCML was attacking everyone. It attacked UNEF for its strategy, social-democrats for keeping workers and students separate, and Herbert Marcuse, whose theories did not interest the working class, the avant-garde of the class struggle. The next day UJCML prevented its members from demonstrating.

10 May

The tenth of May has often been called the night of the barricades. It was a key date in the May 68 movement. At the Paris Peace talks the American Cyrus Vance shook hands with Ma Van Lau, the North Vietnamese delegate. Georges Pompidou was still in Afghanistan, and discussions between the FEN, SNE-sup and UNEF went round and round like a merry-go-round, without any real agreement. The French government wanted assurances that radical militants would not disturb classes, and promised nothing tangible for convicted students. Assurances were not forthcoming.

At six o'clock p.m. the Lion of Belfort was roaring in Denfert-Rochereau Square where a sea of students was on the rampage. The Movement had greatly expanded, for now the original university students had been joined by medical students, law students, high school students and many others. An announcement to the impassioned crowd with a megaphone that the government had not agreed to free the incarcerated students set off a blast of protest: "Free our comrades!" the crowd chanted.

The 22 March Movement and Dany the Red led the way. "Everyone is security," he said. UNEF security had been set aside for the day, which was a bad omen. People with transistor radios cheered when it was announced at 7 p.m. that a recent poll gave tangible proof of the Movement's popularity with the public.

Alain Peyrefitte was meeting with the FEN, Marangé and Daubard. The four condemned students would have to lodge an appeal. The judges would pronounce their verdict soon, so it was no longer a question of amnesty, it was a legal matter. The Sorbonne would be reopened and student identity cards would be checked before setting foot on campus.

The four arrested students had been transformed into martyrs. Neither the crowd nor the student leaders wanted a compromise, they wanted to fight. And so the neighborhood was transformed into a war zone.

Demonstrators resorted once more to the use of one of their favorite symbols: the barricades. From 1830 to 1851 they were regularly used in France by young Republicans like Louis-Auguste Blanqui or François-Vincent Raspail who fought Bourbons and Orléans from the top of barricades. Victor Hugo immortalized them in *Les Misérables* (1862), as did Eugène Delacroix in *Liberty Leading the People* (1830), though his painting is a critique of the revolution and the rabble that he scorned.

Barricades were set up in different places. Everything in the street would be used: cars were overturned, trees cut with chainsaws, barrels and garbage cans piled up, street signs torn down, fires started, streets dug up. . . . Perhaps instinctively, the militants felt the barricades would play a useful role at the bargaining table, or maybe it was just an act of defiance against the authorities.

At a little before 10 p.m. an information flash on the radio announced the creation of the first barricade in Rue Le Golf. By giving an on the spot account, the radio stations were accelerating events. Some militants had transistor radios with them–very popular in the sixties–so they were able to know what was going on in different parts of the neighborhood. Soon barricades were set up in all the streets around the Sorbonne, ten in just one hour. By midnight the

Latin Quarter had been transformed into a fortified camp. Battle lines had been drawn. Behind their barricades, demonstrators exalted. Suddenly, life had greater meaning. A revolution was bigger than life. Fighting a repressive authority, or perceived as such, was more important than anything else. The crowd reveled in the exhilaration of defiance and the infinite strength in numbers. Dany, the radical's *ne plus ultra*, screamed into his megaphone: "The Latin Quarter is yours," and the protestors believed it. But he was not taking any chances and had come to this demonstration with his own personal bodyguard. Lines of demonstrators (or chains) were formed, passing cobblestones from a pile to the throwers. "We form lines the same way we make love," one student quipped. And some of the throwers had great arms; they could have fit into the starting rotation of the Los Angeles Dodgers. The atmosphere was like a carnival, but there was also an anxious feeling of uncertainly in the air, of impending danger.

Reporters became the media's spokesmen for the street drama. Of course the media were excited, too, because they had something to talk about, and they were saying it live. The reporters had become the spokesmen for the demonstrators, and their announcements hit the airwaves like grenades exploding in the night. The radio reports were scary, too, as was the television footage of the events.

Destroying became a game. Destroying for the fun of it, which was easier than building something. Interviews confirmed what Gustave Le Bon had written about crowds: the exalted feeling of power, the lack of rational thought, the potential for violence and destruction, fusion with the mass of militants. "I was happy," said one demonstrator. "I had never felt such a sensation of power and happiness. I was making history, or rather, I was defying it. I was destroying almost with joy. The others no longer existed, though I was obeying the feelings of the crowd. I had the impression of being free and powerful when in fact I was dominated" (DAN 118-19).

Around 10 p.m. a new government compromise was dished out. University president Jean Roche was ready to invite students to discuss reopening the Sorbonne.

UNEF made a declaration concerning the four incarcerated students, stating its promise not to occupy the university, which it could not have really believed in. The problem was that the student union could not speak for the radical militants, namely JCR, 22 March, UJCML. As a matter of fact, the government's message seemed to have little impact on the demonstrators who were not prepared to abandon their well-constructed barricades.

After the government's message, Alain Geismar and the vice president of the Sorbonne, Claude Chalin, exchanged answers by separate radios. The vice president was apparently unaware that his message was being broadcast on the radio. Geismar was speaking from the street where the demonstration was taking place. Chalin received his message via a radio telephone and Radio Television Luxembourg (RTL).

Geismar said he was not ready to go to the Sorbonne under any conditions. The police had to leave and president Roche had to respond to all three student demands. Amnesty for the four incarcerated students had to be granted. Chalin even suggested meeting Geismar where he was, in the street, but the leader of SNE-sup told him not to bother if the third condition could not be met.

At 11:30 p.m. Alain Touraine, professor at Nanterre, who often served as intermediary between protestors and the establishment, had assembled two other professors and three student delegates to attempt to reach an agreement with

Roche. Their goal was to get the police to leave the vicinity of the Sorbonne.

Police chief Jacques Laurent received instructions to take a delegation of protestors to meet with the head of the Sorbonne, who only asked that Daniel Cohn-Bendit not be included in the group because he had to appear before a disciplinary committee. It is logical to assume that there were other reasons for not wanting to see the cantankerous rebel. But chief Laurent recognized Dany from the pictures he had seen in the papers. He objected to letting Dany in to negotiate with Roche, but the professors were fast talkers and said they would go in first, and then let the president decide. Outside the education building, the caretaker let the three professors inside, who immediately asked to let the students come in, too. Roche did not know what Cohn-Bendit looked like, so Dany got in on the sly. While they were negotiating, Pierre Pelletier, Alain Peyrefitte's cabinet director, heard on the radio that a delegation including Daniel Cohn-Bendit had gone inside to see president Roche, and so he informed his minister. Alain Peyrefitte wasted no time in calling Roche and asked him if there was a student with red hair and a plump, round face in the room. Roche had to admit that there was one standing right in front of him. "Well, that's Cohn-Bendit! What's going on?" demanded Peyrefitte. At that point the minister told Roche to stop negotiations immediately. Things were getting crazier than a Laurel and Hardy slapstick.

The delegation was promptly escorted out of the office and into the street, where Dany took advantage of the fiasco to occupy center stage: "What is happening this evening in the street shows that young people everywhere are protesting against a certain kind of society" (DAN 127). His announcement was more revealing than he thought. That was exactly what the demonstrations and the violence were about: young people were protesting against society; against the kind of society they could not believe in, and it was not only happening in France, it was taking place in industrialized nations everywhere.

During the hurried consultations, barricades were being hastily built. The Latin Quarter was a shambles. Christian Fouchet was concerned primarily with one thing: removing the barricades before dawn because of the symbolic effect they had. The barricades symbolized a revolution, and it would be dangerous for the government to let people think there was a revolution going on. That could be interpreted as an invitation for others to join in.

Maurice Grimaud preferred to wait until the last subway train had left, that way the youngest protestors would be home and not behind the barricades.

At 2 a.m. on 11 May the police eagerly moved into action. A squadron of CRS had already charged protestors before orders were given. The last demonstrators to evacuate the barricades reportedly burned the cars in an effort to slow down their attackers, but those claims were refuted by UNEF and SNE-sup. Teargas grenades were shot into the barricades and starting fires, sometimes exploding into the backs of those who fled. Each side was blaming the other for the violence.

The École Normale Supérieure had been transformed into a sort of base for the demonstrators. Dozens if not hundreds of police and protestors needed medical attention.

The protestors' goal was to stay in the neighborhood as long as possible, said Sauvageot. Cohn-Bendit claimed the police were shooting grenades with chlorine gas at demonstrators who could not retreat. He blamed the police for the injuries, arguing that the Latin Quarter was calm before the police attacked. People who lived in the neighborhood did what they could to help the protestors by giving them water or bed sheets soaked in water to protect them from the teargas, small grocers gave what they had in stock, and some bakers gave bread, the traditional French *baguette*. Student popularity had reached its high water mark because in the minds of the public, they were the victims and the policemen and CRS were the aggressors.

The wildest rumors were being spread to discredit the enemy, stories of Professor Jacques Monod, Nobel Prize laureate in medicine, getting a hand ripped off, a pregnant woman being killed, a baby being asphyxiated by the noxious gas. . . . It was a form of propaganda.

Three and a half hours were needed to clear twenty-five to thirty barricades. There were eight barricades in place in Rue Gay-Lussac. Police, like a relentless juggernaut, continued their assault, pursuing their victims, clubbing everyone and everything that got in their way.

A huge barrier was silhouetted in the night at the intersection of Ulm and Claude-Bernard. A conglomerate of objects was piled up: tables, chairs, small cabins from a worksite of the École Normale Supérieure, steel tubes. . . . Booby traps had been put in place, too: barbed wire, puddles of oil and gasoline waiting to be set fire to, nails (JOF 148). Police cautiously decided to stop their assault to eliminate the other nearby barricades first.

When they made their final attack all hell broke loose: those who resisted, including young girls, were trampled, savagely beaten, or had their clothing viciously torn and ripped off. Everyone who was caught was beaten, kicked, punched, gassed, and arrested, and then beaten, kicked and punched again.

"Hey! Isn't the *revolution* beautiful," yelled one protestor from atop a barricade. A revolution was what some were hoping for, anyway. That was why the barricades were set up in the first place, not just to protest against closing the Sorbonne.

At 4 a.m. there were only a handful of barricades left. Teams of CRS pursued small bands of protestors who attempted to find protection in courtyards or apartments. The resistance stood firm until dawn, and the last barricades to hold out were those behind the Panthéon, in the Mouffetard neighborhood. At Contrescarpe Square demonstrators got some assistance from above as inhabitants threw things from their windows at the police. The last barricade to hold out was in Rue Thouin at 5:25 a.m. Five minutes later Dany told the remaining few by radio to disperse (DAN 129). And then it was all over.

11–13 May

The first night of the Paris barricades would determine the orientation of the Movement for the days to come. The violence of the night was dramatically expressed by its numbers: 274 wounded policemen, 18 admitted to hospitals; 116 wounded demonstrators, 36 admitted to hospitals; 60 burned vehicles, 128 were damaged. Some affirmed that people with burned automobiles received no compensation.

What assessment can be made of those events? Public opinion supported the students more than it did the police who were seen as the aggressors, or the government, that appeared to be floundering in its own incompetence. Though the barricades did not last more than a few hours, they helped to galvanize student resistance. It was a battle cry for others to join the revolt against oppression. Students, with growing numbers of youths from the suburbs, rattled the social and educational cages in Paris. Alain Peyrefitte was eager to find a way out of the quagmire and asked James Marangé to contact UNEF. The student position, however, had not changed one iota: their three demands had to be met: open the Sorbonne, evacuate the police from the Latin Quarter, and free all students imprisoned during the demonstrations.

Pierre Messmer, Secretary of Defense, went to the Élysée when the night of turmoil was over to inform general de Gaulle of the situation. He was joined by Louis Joxe and Christian Fouchet (DAN 130). De Gaulle wanted to know if the army was ready, but he was not prepared to use it yet.

About four in the afternoon he met with Louis Joxe, Christian Fouchet and Maurice Grimaud. The negotiations collapsed because the students' demands had not been met. The only way to defuse the protest bomb was to yield to those demands. This line of reasoning seemed to have little effect on the General, who responded by saying "One does not yield to a mob" (DAN 130).

Alain Peyrefitte believed that some sort of compromise had to be made with the students, rather than just giving in to their demands. He proposed a give and take arrangement: the students who were incarcerated would be freed or granted amnesty, but if student violence erupted again, a state of emergency would be declared; police would only be removed from the Latin Quarter when order had been reestablished. More cabinet meetings were to follow with different ministers–Justice, Defense, Interior, Education–in the presence of Prime Minister Pompidou.

Daniel Cohn-Bendit sent a message to the unions calling for a general strike in solidarity with the students. Alain Geismar snuck back to the École Normale Supérieure and his research laboratory in Rue Lhomond. Like other leaders and protestors he was wondering if the army was going to intervene. He left the Latin Quarter very discreetly–hiding in a car–and went to Rue de Solférino. One supposes he was afraid of being arrested, or even worse, in light of the rumors that were circulating about people disappearing. When he was informed that certain government officials were trying to contact him, he replied that he only negotiated with a minister (JOF 152). Knowing that the government was looking bad, he was not in a hurry. The media, cashing in on the violence, had helped to blow the situation sky high.

Maurice Grimaud, for his part, was not totally dissatisfied with the way things were going, though the ghosts of 6

February 1934, were haunting his memory. That was the day of an antiparliamentary demonstration in Paris in front of the National Assembly to protest the firing of prefect Jean Chiappe as a result of the Stavisky affair. At the Place de la Concorde a terrible riot erupted. In all, there were thirty-seven deaths and about two thousand persons injured. Only one person in the forces of law and order died. To this day it is still uncertain what set off the riot and who fired first.

The press, for the most part, condemned the police brutality of the preceding night, and public opinion condemned it as well. Numerous examples were cited of police beating people who were not resisting, who were lying on the ground, who were wounded, who had been arrested in the paddy wagons, young girls and innocent bystanders, in short, anyone who happened to get in the way. Countless cases were reported of broken bones, ribs, and head wounds, injured eyes and damaged lungs from the teargas. The brutality was excessive and it was sadistic.

The CRS attempted to defend itself by pointing the finger at the municipal police officers who, in their opinion, lacked experience to handle those kinds of situations. Despite these claims, eyewitness reports, photographs and films of the events do not exonerate them.

Maurice Grimaud had an old-fashioned and unvarnished analysis of the violence (GRI 169). He gave the incongruous example of one automobilist killing another automobilist because of a dispute over a parking place, or because one driver pulled in front of the other. It goes without saying that people sometimes become maniacs behind the wheel, but justifying sadistic tendencies by saying it was human nature could not guarantee security or establish the moral standards necessary for creating an effective and impassioned police force. The police, he added, were forced to submit to insults and violent acts. So when they got a chance to crack heads, they "enter[ed] the mysterious universe of violence." "I truly think that violence is the price we pay, on both sides, for not being able to kill" (GRI 169). Thus, beating people up, innocent or otherwise, is a substitute for not killing people.

Grimaud's fatalistic and puerile acceptance of police brutality is far from reassuring, and his parochial analysis of the problem probably has not changed in many places. But certainly there are other alternatives to condoning excessive use of force. Maybe those who cannot arrest people without having to beat them up do not belong in uniform. Implicitly, Grimaud was suggesting that citizens should be thankful there were not dozens of deaths. In any event, the morning newspapers let it be known that France disavowed its police, perhaps because the brutality evoked unsavory memories of the Vichy regime.

At noon, the CGT and CFDT called for a general strike for next Monday, 13 May, along with a call to demonstrate in all the large cities. Yet the acute antagonism between students and the CGT could not go unnoticed. Georges Séguy made it perfectly clear that the march should steer clear of the Latin Quarter. Naturally, UNEF and SNE-sup disagreed, and knew it would be difficult to explain that to students.

UNEF was not shy about making demands either: security for the march would be assured by its members only, it would have the exclusive right to publish in the radical paper *Action*, there would be only one leader per organization at the head of the procession, and all the other demonstrators would be students (SEG 26). Georges Séguy got in touch with Eugène Descamps to let him know that he considered those conditions a blatant attempt to "sabotage the march." It was finally decided that security would be handled by all the unions, that nothing would be published, that it would be a union demonstration, and, finally, that there would be three leaders from each organization at the head of the procession (SEG 26).

One other condition added by the head of the CGT was that they did not want any red-haired undesirables up front in the march (DAN 136). Alain Geismar was quick to defend Daniel Cohn-Bendit, stating that he would be up front with the other student leaders, or else there could be no negotiation between students' and workers' unions. Eugène Descamps of the CFDT managed to get Séguy to accept. There was far too much at stake to squelch the collaboration for a mere detail.

Later, student leaders felt they had been in too much of a hurry to contact workers' unions. Negotiating with them was always more complicated it seemed.

After the discussions that afternoon with de Gaulle and his cabinet, Alain Peyrefitte was reassured. The three student demands would be accepted, but with certain conditions, and the Sorbonne would be reopened. He called for a meeting the next morning at nine o'clock with Jean Roche and the deans of the Sorbonne. It was just after 7 pm.

About the same time, Georges Pompidou arrived at Orly, returning from his trip to Iran and Afghanistan, two countries where he hoped to develop relations with France. He had been Prime Minister for six years and had learned a few tricks of the trade while in the political shadow of the General. Pompidou was an important collaborator, perhaps the General's most important collaborator.

When Pompidou stepped off the plane, he had already decided how to handle the situation with the students: reopen the Sorbonne, remove the police, and free the prisoners. It was as simple as that. Peyrefitte wanted to hang on to conditions, but the Prime Minister had already made up his mind.

Moreover, he did not like to do things half way. According to Georges Pompidou, de Gaulle accepted his plan immediately, which is a little hard to believe because he was opposed to reopening the Sorbonne and giving in to rioters.

Pompidou went on television that night at 11:30 p.m., a fact which stressed the urgency of the situation and gave the population what it was hoping for: appeasement, stating that the Sorbonne would be reopened on Monday, and that beginning on that same day the court of appeals could give a verdict on the request for liberation of the condemned students. He arrived at this decision, he said, because of his deep sympathy for the students, and his confidence in their common sense. He also called upon students to disregard the provocations of a few professional agitators and to cooperate with those seeking a peaceful solution (DAN 133). "This appeasement," he asserted, "for my part I am ready."

The Union for a New Republic (UNR)–founded 1 October 1958 to support Charles de Gaulle–was aghast when they heard Pompidou's appeasement speech. They felt he had betrayed not only the police, but the magistracy, the government, and the General.

Pompidou's allocution probably appeased the public to some extent. UNEF, for its part, had taken a less moderate tone when it said: "Our efforts must lead to a radical critique of universities and call into question the government, of which the repressive nature is clear to all" (DAN 133).

University professors were criticized by some for being poorly informed. Many were unaware of the revolutionary inspiration of the student movement and had little or no knowledge of de Gaulle's plan for being firm. Probably few if any were aware that non-students were participating in the demonstrations and riots.

The workers' unions agreed that police brutality must be

denounced. Eugène Descamps, General Secretary of the CFDT, stated that the student crisis had become so acute, that his union could no longer ignore the problem. The SGEN and the Federation of Metal Workers had informed him of the police brutality. At the same time, union leaders were stunned by the immaturity of some student leaders who appeared to be playing at being adults.

Union protest against police brutality took the form of a twenty-four hour strike, and a march. There were many strikers in the public service sector, the SNCF, RATP, EDF, but fewer in private industry.

The demonstration succeeded in mobilizing a large crowd: students of all categories–university, high school, École Normale–gathered at Verdun Square. The demonstrators were described by many as joyful and enthusiastic, no doubt because of the barricades on Friday night. During the assembly Daniel Cohn-Bendit demanded the resignation of the Minister of the Interior and the prefect, and the creation of a tribunal made up of common people to oversee police activity and judge unwarranted behavior. Needless to say, his demands did not get very far.

At 3 p.m. the procession of demonstrators began marching. There were quite a few red flags, and at the head of the demonstration was a banderole with the words: "Students, Teachers, Workers, standing together." Daniel Cohn-Bendit, Jacques Sauvageot, Alain Geismar, Eugène Descamps, Georges Séguy, and an FO member were up front; Waldeck Rochet, Georges Marchais, Guy Mollet, Pierre Mendès France, François Mitterrand and other party leaders were further behind in the procession (DAN 136-37).

At Denfert-Rochereau Square a CGT striker announced the end of the march and the dispersion of the strikers. That was a cue for Dany the Red to yell into his megaphone: "Go to the Champ-de-Mars." It was not too hard for him and other students to get past CGT security. Thousands of students poured into Raspail and Montparnasse Boulevards.

A driver of a police emergency van apparently lost his head and nearly plowed into some demonstrators. He was yanked out of the vehicle and beaten up, and the windows of the vehicle were smashed. Another officer took out his revolver and shot three times in the air. Pierre Cot intervened in time to prevent the officers from being lynched (DAN 137). Maurice Grimaud gives a different account of the incident. An emergency vehicle, he says, was taking an injured child to a hospital and took the shortest route to get there quicker. The driver was stopped by security for the demonstration, which let the van pass when they understood what the driver was doing. Further on, however, demonstrators did not know what the vehicle was doing and only saw it heading for them at a high speed and stopped it. Some excited youths tried to pull the officers out of the vehicle. Thinking that his life was threatened, the policeman drew his gun and shot in the air to make the demonstrators back off. Police assistance was asked for and a group of policemen that had received the message by radio would have intervened with their guns drawn to assist an officer in distress. Fortunately, Pierre Cot, a friend of the prefect, called him to let him know that the officers would be protected, but insisted that reinforcements not be sent, since that could only aggravate an already tense situation (GRI 184-85).

The estimations for the demonstration were certainly exaggerated, though there was indeed a very large crowd. The CGT said there were 800,000, the CFDT said a million. The Office of French Radio and Television Diffusion (ORTF) said there were 171,000, a number that the demonstrators found ridiculous.

Students and other young protestors were letting themselves be deluded by their dreams, by their quixotic fantasies of toppling the government, hoping that the working class would follow the Movement, but in France in 1968, the working class meant the CGT primarily, and the CGT could not put up with unshaven, slovenly, long-haired radicals, especially when they had red hair. Georges Séguy did not like the idea of young radicals trying to establish themselves as the "guiding force and brains of the working class struggle" (SEG 25).

The Odéon Theatre

The Odéon theatre is located in the sixth arrondissement in Odéon Square. It has a long and impressive history. The troupe of actors known as the Comédie Française settled in the new theatre on 16 February 1782. Queen Marie-Antoinette inaugurated the sumptuous theatre on 9 April 1782. Sarah Bernhardt is said to have begun her theatrical career there, performing *Phaedra* by Racine for the holiday of the Emperor on 15 August 1866. Jean-Louis Barrault, one of France's finest actors and pantomimes, was director of the Odéon from 1959 to 1968, but he lost his directorship because of the events in May.

On 15 May 1968, the historic theatre was overrun by students–some say a thousand, some say three thousand. A little before midnight Paul Taylor's ballet company had just finished its performance. Carrying a banderole, militants galloped up the stairs. There was no conceivable way of keeping them out. After the demonstration on Monday, 13 May, some artists, writers, painters and film makers got together and discussed occupying the Odéon to protest against "consumer art" (DAN 153), a subject that had inspired Andy Warhol. The committee organizing the idea was attempting to rally students to their cause. Jean-Jacques Lebel, artist, writer and organizer of happenings, promoted the project. He organized about seventy happenings on several continents, working with people like Yoko Ono, John Lennon's wife. Lebel also translated the works of the Beats, notably William Burroughs, Allen Ginsberg, Gregory Corso, as well as the poetry of Lawrence Ferlinghetti and Michael McLure.

Jean-Louis Barrault, warned about the invasion, tried to mollify the motley crowd of revolutionaries. "I fully understand your aspirations. . . . The Odéon Theatre of France is also an international theatre where plays from around the world are performed. . . . Let them express themselves freely," he pleaded, but nobody was listening to the celebrated mime of *Children of Paradise*. Madeleine Renaud, gifted actress, did not get very far with the youths either. "The Odéon had performed the plays of Genet, Ionesco, Beckett. . . . Our theatre is not a bourgeois theatre . . . you'd be better advised to occupy other theatres. . . ." But Ionesco *was* considered bourgeois and irrelevant by the many youths in the theater that evening. Censorship exists on both sides of the political spectrum.

On 15 May the 22 March Movement declared that "the occupation of the Odéon [was] an act of revolutionary agitation." In the Office of the Commission of Information of the Odéon [*sic*], a reporter asked the students who were now in charge several questions. Why was the Odéon taken? Who took it? Now that you've taken it, what are you going to do? A communiqué was read in response to those questions. "The 22 March Movement called for the creation of revolutionary action committees at all workplaces. A certain number of artists, actors, students and workers have decided to create a revolutionary action committee at the sites of bourgeois culture. The Odéon was not chosen to personally attack the company of actors but so that the Theatre of France stops being a theatre for an undetermined period. Beginning 16 May 1968, it becomes a meeting place for workers, students, artists and actors; secondly, a creative revolutionary committee room to begin reflecting on our refusal to produce performances as merchandise; thirdly, an uninterrupted meeting place, beginning this evening at midnight."

On 16 May a black flag for anarchism and a red flag for communism adorned the pediment of the theatre. A large streamer read: "Students-Workers, the Odéon is Open." Dany the Red was there to maintain the occupation. The theatre, he said, was a "symbol of bourgeois and Gaullist culture. . . . We must consider the theatre as an instrument to combat the bourgeoisie." Jean-Louis Barrault, overwhelmed by the radicals' impromptu performance of the absurd, was still vainly attempting to appease them: "I completely agree with Monsieur (indicating Cohn-Bendit), Barrault is no longer director of this theatre, but just an actor like the others. Barrault is dead." How little did he suspect at the time that his words would become a self-fulfilling prophecy.

On 22 May general de Gaulle refused to send the CRS to have the Odéon evacuated–probably fearing the place would be destroyed–but he demanded that the electricity be shut off. Jean-Louis Barrault, who was already in André Malraux's disfavor, refused to comply. Other striking theatres closed their doors in May, including the Theatre of the Gymnasium (Théâtre du Gymnase) and the Comédie Française, while the TNP was placed under the protection of its employees.

On 23 May the Cabinet of the Minister of Cultural Affairs formally recorded Barrault's disobedience and published a communiqué in the press disavowing his conduct. Barrault answered the Minister, André Malraux, in the style of the times: "Servant yes, lackey no!"

The prefect Maurice Grimaud oversaw the evacuation of the Odéon on 14 June, which was done without violence. Jean-Louis Barrault refused to make a statement, knowing he had been abandoned by his friends in the Ministry. Inside, the theatre was a shambles and in need of vast repairs that must have cost a fortune. It had become a favorite squat for the down-and-out, dealers, alcoholics, and a host of derelicts. The "security" during the last few weeks of the occupation was taken care of by the "black jacket" brigade, so called because of the black leather jackets they wore (GOFF 94-95). They came from Belleville and Gennevilliers and else-where in the Parisian suburbs where it could be dangerous to walk alone. Some of them had exotic names like "the Angel of Death" or "Rocky." They were present on the first night of the barricades, but there were a lot more of them on 24 May. The "black jackets" were also present on the occupied campuses, giving them an aspect not dissimilar to a den of thieves. There were two Hungarian emigrants, a former legionnaire, and a Jew from the Six Day War in security, too. They spent their time in the Odéon making Molotov cocktails and looking for spies and snitches. They pillaged what they could, the costumes and the accessories mostly.

Strikes: 13-16 May

In 1967 and 1968 there was a recession in France, bringing with it a decline in prosperity and the resultant feelings of uncertainty. The general increase in salaries had slowed down and was officially a mere 7% above the cost of living, the minimum wage (SMIG) only 4%. Before 1966, manpower was lacking in French industry and so it was imported from Algeria, Spain, Portugal, Greece, or the Near East. But with an increase in unemployment, foreign manpower was no longer a vital necessity, and could even beget racial tension as competition for jobs increased. Baby-boomers who were looking for work found it difficult to find, and young applicants with qualifications found it difficult to find work that matched their credentials. From 1 December 1967 to 1 December 1968, there were 100,000 more unemployed.

The strike at Saviem, a company owned by Renault, seemed to exemplify the industrial situation in France at the time. Its 4,800 employees at Blainville-sur-Orne assembled trucks. For the most part, the workers there were young men from rural areas who found their jobs boring, with no chance of advancement. The exams they took to acquire qualifications turned out to be a waste of time. 6% of the workforce belonged to a union, primarily the CFDT. Workers lodged numerous complaints with their delegates: advancement was determined not by technical competence but by toadying, bill sticking was censored, and dismissals were linked to hiring lower paid workers to replace those who had previously been fired (DAN 168).

To save money, the company bosses reduced employee working hours, so the workers had less money to live on. Saviem did this in June 1967 and also in January 1968. Tired of having their complaints fall on the deaf ears of management, workers of the company's three factories went on strike on 23 January 1968, blocking the entrance to the plant. On the 24th of January the CRS attacked the strikers, who fought back with stones and boards. Several thousand protestors demonstrated in Caen on the 26th, with the protest ending in a riot. The forces of law and order used 630 teargas grenades and 85 offensive grenades; 9 persons were hospitalized, 113 had minor wounds; 85 persons (mostly students) were arrested, and 6 were given minor sentences. On the 29th gendarmes prevented strikers from picketing. The sad conflict came to an end on 5 February 1968, without a single demand of the strikers being met (DAN 169). This could in many ways be described as the *status quo* in French industry, and explained the mounting feeling of enmity and dissatisfaction that was endemic in many factories.

On Tuesday, 14 May, Sud-Aviation in Bougenais–today the company is called Aérospatial–declared a strike and the factory was occupied. Pierre Duvochel and some executives were sequestered in the offices of the CGT at the factory. Doors were tied shut with cables. Union security kept the plant well-guarded in case the police tried to force their way in. This was the first wildcat strike in May, but it would not be the last. The demonstrations and riots in Paris helped to create the climate necessary to shut the factory down, and the militancy of Yvon Rocton and Alexandre Hébert helped to create the atmosphere inside the factory that was needed to launch a successful strike.

On Monday, 13 May, the Renault factory in Cléon, near Rouen, went on strike, with a turnout of 30%. Union delegates asked to meet with the company bosses, but the executives refused, claiming that they would not meet with them under duress. Those in charge of the factory blocked the door with metal bars to prevent strikers from forcing their way into the offices. When union leaders saw that, they decided to do the same thing, locking everyone in until management agreed to meet with union delegates. At midnight, the director finally decided to talk and listen to workers' demands, which were: recognition of trade union membership in the factory, return to a forty hour week without a loss in wages, and a minimum wage of one thousand francs. The director and his chief executives were not allowed to leave until Saturday, 18 May, when they began a hunger strike.

On Thursday, 16 May, spontaneous strikes erupted in Flins and the other factories of Renault France, including Orléans, le Mans and Sandouville. Other companies were affected as well, such as Lockheed and Unilec.

But the strike at Boulogne-Billancourt in the afternoon set the general strike in motion. Things would not start to return to normal again until the first week of June.

Before implicating itself in a vast general strike, the CGT wanted to see how things would go with the French National Railway Corporation (SNCF), which was suppressing jobs at the rate of one thousand a month, despite the fact that railway traffic was increasing. The turnout for the strike on Monday, 13 May, was rather weak, with some 90,000 strikers, but things would accelerate in the days to come. By Saturday, 18 May, the strike had gained ground, and by Sunday, 19 May, the railway network was paralyzed.

By Friday, 17 May, there were some 300,000 workers on strike in France. On the eighteenth the SNCF, postal services and telecommunications went on strike, not to mention numerous smaller corporations and businesses. Union leaders claimed there were two million workers on strike. By Monday, 20 May, there were more than seven million strikers. When the sorting centers and bank services of the post office went on strike, the other employees there did not have much choice but to follow.

Electricity of France (EDF) did not go on strike because the CGT wanted to keep it out of the movement for the simple reason that the consequences would be catastrophic for the nation, and a strike there would have undertones of a national insurrection. Though employees remained on the job, they took control of different sites.

Georges Pompidou and the Crisis

The French government had a decision to make. Should president de Gaulle maintain his trip to Romania or not? He was scheduled to leave early Tuesday morning, 14 May. However, the demonstration the previous day made him have second thoughts. The Minister of the Interior was against his leaving. The Prime Minister felt it was better to go. It was finally decided that it would be better not to change everything at the last minute. Later, he would justify his maintaining the trip by saying it would help to develop relations between East and West for peace in the world.

Georges Pompidou was a man of his word, but he may have been taken advantage of because of it. Students that were arrested on the first night of the barricades were released on Sunday, 12 May. On Monday, 13 May, the court of appeals gave suspended sentences to those who had been sentenced to prison. Early that same day the CRS, gendarmerie and police evacuated the Latin Quarter and the Sorbonne was reopened. It appeared to be a generous gesture. But now the government had to tackle the crisis head on.

Early in the morning at Matignon, Georges Pompidou met with the Minister of the Interior Christian Fouchet, the prefect Maurice Grimaud, the Secretary of Defense Pierre Messmer, Director of the Gendarmerie Jean-Claude Périer, Director of the Prime Minister's Cabinet Michel Jobert, and Cabinet Director Pierre Somveille. It was a meeting of "persons in charge of law and order and Ministers concerned with the strikes." This special cabinet would meet every day until the end of the crisis. Officially its function was to help the population cope with the strikes and ensure the continuity of the Republic.

The Prime Minister was in a quandary over the current imbroglio. There was not much he could do against the general strike. Sending the police would only have aggravated an already complex situation. The popularity of the student movement had to some extent handcuffed him.

Seeing that students were able to get a voice, workers, who had been waiting for years to give voice to their grievances, took advantage of the auspicious situation to occupy factories, go on strike and demand higher wages and better working conditions.

There are several ways of influencing public opinion, and one way of doing that is by using fear. By showing that the country was headed for anarchy, foreign influence, civil war and maybe a *coup d'état*, the government could change public opinion in its favor. Fear was something the average citizen could understand without having to think or analyze. But some sort of tool had to be found.

On Thursday, 16 May, Georges Pompidou gave an unscheduled allocution on television at 9:30 p.m. The tone of his message was grave. He warned the public against certain extremists who sought to make disorder widespread in an effort to destroy the nation and a free society. The government, he declared, must and would defend the Republic. He told students not to follow the dictates of provocateurs who were disinterested in the vast majority of students. The government was prepared to listen to legitimate demands and asked students not to ruin their chances by acting unlawfully. The government would do its duty, he affirmed, but it needed public support. The public could do that by rejecting anarchy. Prior to the legislative elections in June, he would tell voters they could stop anarchy, subversion and totalitarianism by voting for the Union for the Defense of the Republic (UDR).

In the first week of May, Michel Honorin, a well-known journalist, produced a documentary about the student revolt for the popular television program called "Cinq colonnes à la une." The directors and editors showed it to Jean-Pierre Hutin, adviser to Georges Gorse, Minister of Information. Honorin's footage would not be broadcast and was censored because Hutin thought it depicted protesting students too favorably, so it would be bad for public opinion. Honorin made a scene when he was told about scrapping his footage, but that was not going to change anything, and the documentary was put on ice indefinitely.

On Monday evening, after the Sunday demonstration, newsmen and journalists were scandalized by the biased report given by the 8 p.m. news broadcast, the primary newscast of the day.

The next day a committee for the freedom of information was set up. A few days later the Office of French Radio and Television Diffusion (ORTF) went on strike. Minimum service was assured by a team supporting the government's viewpoint, though many criticized the amateurishness of the programs.

Because more and more public services and workers were going on strike, Christian Fouchet asked general de Gaulle to return to France immediately. The presidential Caravelle landed at Orly on Saturday, 18 May, at 10:30 p.m.

Sunday, 19 May, Georges Pompidou, Christian Fouchet, Alain Peyrefitte, Georges Gorse, Maurice Grimaud and Jacques Foccart were summoned for a meeting at the Élysée Palace in the early afternoon. The General was not happy because things had not been going the way they were supposed to. Student radicals had made a mockery of Pompidou's generosity, and subversion was taking hold of France's institutions. De Gaulle felt the occupation of the Odéon was an insult to his government and the Republic because it had nothing to do with the student demands.

De Gaulle wanted the Sorbonne and the Odéon to be evacuated immediately, that very night. Those sitting around him were stunned, they knew that could not be done peaceably. Fouchet and Grimaud told him it would be impossible for the Sorbonne, so the General reluctantly acquiesced, but he still wanted the subversives out of the Odéon. Maurice Grimaud consulted his collaborators. There were a lot of people in the Odéon, hundreds, and if they knew the police were coming, they would bring hundreds more in. The police even studied a plan to raid the theatre from the sewers, but that idea was abandoned. The Sorbonne and the Odéon Theatre would not be freed until the next month.

As Georges Pompidou left the Élysée Palace, reporters were eager to know what had been decided. The Prime Minister summarized de Gaulle's ideas succinctly by saying, "Reform yes, anarchy no."

22-24 May

The omnipresence of the general strike had been making itself felt. The economic activity of the country had come to a standstill. The streets were filled with mountains of garbage that kept piling up, most gas stations were empty and if you were lucky enough to find one open, you had to pay through the nose, banks were limiting withdrawals to 1,000 francs, long lines formed in front of stores, the Cannes Film Festival was closed because the actors' union voted to go on strike. . . . People were afraid that things would get worse before they got better.

High schools, many of which were empty, had found a new watchword: "autodiscipline." This idea, it was argued, would replace adult authority, but for many it was seen as a short cut for rejecting all forms of discipline. Some saw it as a way of expressing their freedom, though they probably failed to realize that "freedom" is intrinsically linked to responsibility.

While in Frankfort, Dany the Red was banned from France on 21 May 1968. Needless to say, the Movement was in an uproar. French authorities used the law to remove a person whom they considered *persona non grata*. "Our goal," he boasted, "is not just to get rid of de Gaulle and his government, but the whole system. The French government should mobilize the entire French army to keep me out of France" (KER 67). While haranguing a crowd of students in Berlin he reportedly said: "The Tricolor was made to be ripped up, to make a red flag" (CHA). But that did not stop

Dany, who had the chutzpa to sneak back to Paris on 28 May with a fairly elaborate disguise. He was well-advised because customs officers were on the lookout for chubby young men with red hair. Dany went to a meeting at the Sorbonne where he was praised as a hero, and it seems he protested in a demonstration, too. The attractive and extremely popular actress Marie-France Pisier hid the outspoken rebel in her car and drove him to Paris.

The General Intelligence Directorate had been watching every move Dany made for some time. "A briefing note was transmitted to the Ministry of the Interior stating that Daniel Cohn-Bendit crossed the German border last night, in Forbach, heading for Frankfort in a vehicle with license plate number 5147V92. The vehicle used by Daniel Cohn-Bendit, a Citroën ID 19, belongs to a private company by the name of Verjat. It was rented on the 20th of May at about 6 p.m. by a telephone call coming from the [offices of the] magazine *Paris Match*. The driver of the vehicle, Paul Tora, employed by Verjat, was directed to transport his passengers: Daniel Cohn-Bendit, Jean Durieux, journalist, and Georges Melet, photograph" (CHA).

At the same time the National Center for French Employers (CNPF) was looking for a way to end the crisis, because they were losing money like everyone else with the general strike. André Barjonet, an economist for the CGT, received a call from an unknown collaborator of Paul Huvelin, president of the CNPF. Employers were ready to negotiate with people acting in good faith. Barjonet informed his boss as soon as he could (JOF 245).

As fate would have it, general de Gaulle gave an allocution on television the second night of the barricades. Students learned a couple of days before that their revolutionary hero, Dany the Red, had been banned from entering France.

Protestors expressed their anger in the streets, protesting for three straight days, on the twenty-second to the twenty-fourth.

General Demettre went to see Maurice Grimaud to explain the situation concerning the mobile police squadrons. It was time, he said, for the government to make up its mind: "The police can hold on to Paris, or they can hold on to artichokes from Brittany." The general was fond of rural metaphors. His units were exhausted, getting only five to six hours of sleep a night, if that (GRI 228-29). Maurice Grimaud had 58 mobile squadrons at his disposal at that time (with 75 men in a squadron).

Christian Fouchet called the prefect on Wednesday, 22 May. He was well aware that the decision to ban Cohn-Bendit from France would excite an already wound up youth. He had not asked Grimaud's opinion before making the decision; as Minister of the Interior, it was for him to decide. He confessed that he was ready to arrest other "agitators" if necessary to control the situation. The question was probably not if the demonstrators would be inflamed, but how inflamed they could get. But apart from that, the idea of arresting those who criticized the government cast a forbidding shadow on the principle of freedom of speech in a democracy.

Jacques Sauvageot of UNEF called for students to demonstrate on the twenty-second. Police guarded bridges to keep demonstrators from going to the right bank of the Seine. Red flags and black flags headed the procession, which the police interpreted as ultra-revolutionary. When Sauvageot surprisingly left the demonstration at 8:30 p.m., Alain Geismar took over. The group had grown to about 7,000 demonstrators at that point.

Naturally the police had carefully placed its informants

in the procession, and they used their small radio-transceivers that they kept hidden to let the police command room know what the demonstrators were going to do (GRI 231). This was common practice in the police, though most students seemed unaware of the fact.

Christian Fouchet, piqued by the criticism of his handling of the riots, was afraid the protestors would get to the Bourbon Palace, home of the National Assembly. To prevent this, a formidable police barrage of 1,500 officers kept the crowd at bay. Geismar wanted a public debate in front of the National Assembly, and a few, very few, representatives did say a few words to the demonstrators. But soon Geismar was vociferating again and telling the crowd to return to the Latin Quarter.

The most excited demonstrators–many of whom were not students–went on a rampage throughout the night, and tried, but failed, to burn down the Association for the Support of General de Gaulle in Rue Solférino. These groups also tried to set fire to the police station in the fifth arrondissement. Things did not return to normal until a little before 6 a.m. the next morning.

UNEF and SNE-sup held a meeting in Rue Monsieur-le-Prince in the late morning and decided to organize a large demonstration in support of Cohn-Bendit on 24 May. The more extreme elements in the crowd, however, could not wait till the next day and decided to demonstrate right away. Fouchet agreed to let them demonstrate in the Latin Quarter, convinced the police squadrons stationed on bridges and embankments could control the situation.

At 5 p.m. about 2,000 youths had gathered at Saint-Michel Square, and by 7:30 p.m. the number had increased to about 5,000. Maurice Grimaud says the crowd was particularly boisterous and aggressive (GRI 234). Suddenly the strike action was given without the police knowing by whom, and trouble erupted. Fires were lit everywhere, and it seemed as though destruction was the basic form of protest. UNEF and SNE-sup leaders arrived at 7:45 p.m. to try and calm things down. They wanted people to go home and come back the next day for the big demonstration. This seemed to be a lost cause, since, for the most part, union leaders were ignored. When firemen arrived to put out the fires, they were attacked by the demonstrators. This was very unusual because firefighters are highly respected in Paris. Security forces for UNEF and SNE-sup did their best to protect them.

At 9 p.m. demonstrators were tearing apart Saint-André-des-Arts Square, a popular meeting place in the Latin Quarter. As a result, Maurice Grimaud ordered police to clear the area. Provocations and fights would continue in the neighborhood until about 11 p.m. The usual patterns were being repeated, though they had nothing to do with students' or workers' demands: grilles were broken and used as projectiles, street lamps were broken, signs torn down, and barricades reappeared in the streets of Paris, some of which, like the ones at Luxembourg Station, at the corner of Saint-Jacques and Saint-Germain, were very large. Things had gotten totally out of control.

At 9:50 p.m. Alain Geismar told rioters not to attack the police, who said they would leave the Latin Quarter if the vandalism and aggression stopped. Maurice Grimaud said he would have liked to broadcast that information by radio, but it was 11 p.m. and the government had outlawed direct transmissions over the radio after eleven o'clock. The idea being that direct reporting overdramatized events, and that excited many demonstrators, making them commit violent acts.

Barricades were still being erected at Saint-Germain and Monge-Écoles, which meant that streets were still being torn up, trees cut, cars overturned and property destroyed, so the police intervened. Shortly before midnight, UNEF, SNE-sup and 22 March said they were not at all responsible for the barricades and the disorder that night (GRI 236). The unruly crowd had a mind of its own. From midnight to 3 a.m. police fought with rioters to take control of the barricades. At 1:20 a.m. Christian Fouchet sent a communiqué stating that some demonstrators were not students. It is probably fair to say that most of the violence was caused by nonstudents. It was mayhem for the sake of mayhem. Gangs of youths from the suburbs had gone to Paris to riot and vandalize. Some demonstrators also believed that by causing disorder, they could incite people to riot, and that would or could lead to a revolution. The fantasy of a revolution was in the minds of many demonstrators, though in truth it was chimerical.

The events of 24 May would be much more violent than the two previous nights.

Two demonstrations were announced: one by the students and one by the workers. The student demonstration began at the Lyon Station at 7 p.m. The other demonstration was organized by the CGT, which had previously denounced the leftwing provocations of the radical students. The workers' demonstration would be in the suburbs and also in Paris.

It was not difficult to understand that the police were mainly concerned with the demonstration at Lyon Station. Experience had shown that the CGT remained in control of its processions. It was careful to organize its march so that it would not come into contact with the students that day. The CGT had three large demonstrations in the suburbs: Gennevilliers, Boulogne, and Nanterre; and two processions in Paris: one starting at Balard Square and proceeding to Austerlitz

Station, the other from the Bastille to Haussmann Boulevard. In Paris there were from seven to ten thousand demonstrators for each march, which is to say they were very small for the powerful French union, sometimes capable of assembling hundreds of thousands of marchers.

The CGT clearly sought to dissociate itself from the student demonstration and show its strength for future negotiations. Séguy candidly made his position clear to the press: no limitless strikes envisioned, and the social movement in progress should be controlled by the workers rather than by the students. When someone asked about Daniel Cohn-Bendit, his response was: "Cohn-Bendit, who is that?"

About 7 p.m. there was a huge crowd of demonstrators in front of Lyon Station, an estimated 25,000, mostly made up of students and workers, but also "Loulous," the roughnecks from the "zone" who were carrying sticks, bicycle chains and sling-shots.

Maurice Grimaud said the gathering would be tolerated, but would not allow a march through Paris. When the demonstration was over, dispersion must take place at the station, not someplace else. He was afraid of what such a large crowd of aggressive youths would do if they went on a rampage through the city, particularly the youths from the suburbs who had no allegiance to a union or its leaders.

When the talks were concluded, there was a call to march west in the direction of the Halles and the Bourse. Police were opposed to that. Several thousand demonstrators headed towards the Bastille, but they were met by the police and could not get by. That is when they started digging up the street and building barricades with the cobblestones. From Lyon Station to the Bastille, barricades and obstacles were set up. The police expected that and had bulldozers ready to break down the barriers, but that was easier said than done because the youths were violent and aggressive.

As usual, police were bombarded with stones and anything that could be thrown; they responded with teargas grenades, offensive grenades, and fire hose trucks that were successful in clearing out the area.

At 11 p.m. police controlled the neighborhood, but police stations in the eleventh and twelfth arrondissements were attacked by rioters. A group of several thousand demonstrators managed to get past the police and continue west. A fire was started at the Bourse, probably because it symbolized capitalism, and firemen were lapidated when they tried to extinguish it, but they were able to extinguish the fire without much difficulty.

Extensive use of teargas and fire hoses allowed the forces of law and order to clear the area around the Bourse, Rue Réaumur, 4-Septembre, the Banque, and the Opéra Square, though it took them fifty minutes to do so. The chief of police in charge of operations there said it took so long because of the violence of the "young hoodlums."

In the neighborhood of the Halles windows were smashed, fires lit, and the judicial police station set on fire. This was the first time that Parisians on that side of the Seine witnessed gratuitous violence. They were shocked to see hundreds of youths running through the streets, screaming slogans in the blazing night and vandalizing property. Few, if any, dared to tell them to stop, and it is not difficult to imagine why.

But the most violent riots occurred in the Latin Quarter. The violence began early at Saint-Michel Square, about 6:30 p.m. By 9 p.m. several thousand youths were busily constructing barricades on Saint-Michel Boulevard and the Rue Saint-Jacques. Trees were cut down with chain saws–130 trees in all–signs were torn down, cars were overturned, streets dug up to remove the cobblestones. . . . Garbage collectors were on strike so garbage was piled up on the sidewalk and in the street–that gave the rioters plenty of things to set on fire.

It was not until 11 p.m. that peace was restored to Saint-Michel Square, but there were still other barricades that needed to be cleared.

It was not unusual for some groups to attack police stations. Central Police Station in the fifth arrondissement in Panthéon Square was besieged by violent youths that did not seem to be afraid of anything. A passerby told officer Boucheny, the policeman in charge, that violent demonstrators were headed that way. The windows were immediately shut, the metal door to the entrance was closed, and policemen outside were warned to go inside for protection.

When the mob arrived the cars in the parking lot were stoned and burned with Molotov cocktails (GRI 244). The fire from the burning vehicles was so intense that it threatened to consume the entire building, with the officers inside. Assistance to the station was delayed because of the barricades and obstacles in the Latin Quarter. Cars were systematically burned there when demonstrators were forced to abandon a barricade, and there is still a debate as to who set them on fire. The police station was finally saved by a unit that arrived in time, going by the Rue du Cardinal Lemoine and the Rue Clovis.

One by one the barricades in the Latin Quarter were removed, and in the early dawn a fragile calm was restored.

The new tactic employed by the demonstrators was to divide themselves into small mobile guerilla groups that pestered the police with the rapid construction of barricades and other obstacles. The "Loulous" from the "zone" had converged with the students, though their goals, if they can be called that, were to destroy property. Vandalism outside of the Latin Quarter was becoming more widespread. The police used bulldozers, large amounts of teargas, fire hoses, radio contact, and, at close quarters, nightsticks to beat the persons they managed to catch. All too often they were innocent victims or persons who did not pose a threat.

The second night of the barricades marked the death of the Philippe Mathérion, the first mortal victim of May 68. He was found near a barricade with a very serious wound in his chest. According to an online article published by *L'Express* on 9 April 1998, entitled "Mai 68: Nouveaux témoignages," Philippe, twenty-six at the time, received a grenade fragment in the chest which resulted in internal bleeding. Medical assistance took too long to get there, and when it finally arrived it was too late. Who fired the grenade? The Police? Someone else? Philippe's father said his son was not a radical leftist and did not want him classified as such. As a result, his death was not used to accuse the police.

For three weeks in France, violence was occurring in the streets of the city, transformed into a sort of guerilla street theatre. There were nine days of violence. The cause of the violence during the first days of May–the 3rd, 6th, 7th, and 10th–was the evacuation of the Sorbonne, and the arrests of students. Prohibiting Daniel Cohn-Bendit from entering France was the cause of another phase of rioting that occurred on the 22nd, 23rd and 24th of May. The death of Gilles Tautin, who drowned in the Seine River when he tried to get away from the CRS in Meulan, was another cause (GRI 258-60).

Statistics for 24 May help to appreciate the extent of the mayhem: 212 policemen were injured, 652 demonstrators were arrested, of which 390 were nonstudents; the fire department received 350 calls to combat fires. It is difficult to know how many students were injured because they were afraid to report their injuries to the police. Violent confrontations occurred in the provinces, too, notably in Bordeaux, Strasbourg, Rennes and especially Lyon, resulting in hundreds of wounded persons.

On 24 May police chief René Lacroix died in Lyon. It had long been claimed by authorities that he was crushed to death by a truck when rioters locked its gas pedal. This was contradicted by an intern at Edouard Herriot Hospital who testified that the Police chief died of a heart attack. While messaging Lacroix's heart, the intern fractured several of his ribs. The intern said that he testified in court when he heard there was a trial with regards to the death of René Lacroix (BUR).

On Friday evening 24 May at 8 p.m. Charles de Gaulle appeared on television to address the public. The crisis in France had gotten worse since 13 May due to a series of strikes and occupied factories involving millions of workers, and resulting in the paralysis of the country. The first duty of the government was to assure the elementary existence of the nation. De Gaulle declared himself ready to undertake the reforms needed, and this would necessarily require the participation of everyone.

The political, economic and social obstacles the country faced needed to be overcome. The university crisis was the result of the institution's inability to adapt itself to the modern needs of the nation. Many other sectors of society had been affected as a result. France, he warned, must solve these problems to avoid the odious perspective of a civil war. The university system must be reformed to assure the future of the nation's youth in a modern, industrialized society.

He asked the people, as he had in 1961 and 1962, to give

him the necessary mandate to accomplish those tasks. This would be done in the form of a referendum, which he qualified as the most direct and democratic way to decide. If the nation voted "no," de Gaulle would resign as president of the Republic.

The speech was succinct, though he did evoke the essential problems that needed to be taken care of. It was criticized because of its brevity and lack of explication. Some found it uninspired and banal. In practice it had little impact if any on the situation, and students were more violent that night than they had been before.

Some of de Gaulle's more vehement critics were union leaders and naturally the political opposition. Nothing was said about worn out structures or the specific examples of immediate problems concerning wages or unemployment. "The plebiscite," said Pierre Mendès France, "is not something you discuss, but something we combat."

25-31 May

Rue de Grenelle passes through several neighborhoods in Paris, including Saint-Germain-des-Prés and Saint-Thomas d'Aquin. It got its name from the old village of Grenelle. It is the site of several remarkable buildings, some of which date back to the seventeenth century. Several ministries are located in this street.

After the riots on Friday, 24 May, and president de Gaulle's speech in the evening, Georges Pompidou decided to plunge ahead with negotiations. Jacques Legrand informed the unions that discussions would begin the very next day, on Saturday, 25 Mai. The government did not have much to lose. Naturally, the Minister of Finance, Michel Debré, was affected, but he was not in favor of granting large concessions, so Pompidou preferred to direct the negotiations alone, without a troublesome colleague putting a damper on things (DAN 244). Pompidou did all the talking for the government.

Nine delegations had gathered at 127 Rue de Grenelle in the historic Hôtel du Châtelet (built from 1770 to 1776), which housed the Ministry of Social Affairs. For the government: Georges Pompidou, Jean-Marcel Jeanneney (Minister of Social Affairs), Jacques Chirac (Secretary of State for Social Affairs), Édouard Balladur; CNPF: Paul Huvelin; CNPME: Gustave Deleau, Daniel Gauban, Aimé d'Oiron; CGT: Georges Séguy, Benoît Frachon, André Berteloot, Henri Krasucki, René Buhl, Jean-Louis Moynot; CFDT: Eugène Descamps, René Bonéty, Jean Maire, Paul Caspard, François Lagandré, René Mathevet; CGT-FO: André Bergeron, Roger Louet, Pierre Tribié, Robert Degris, Antoine Laval; CFTC: Joseph Sauty, Jacques Tessier; CGC: André Malterre, Roger Millot; FEN: James Marangé, Georges Aulong, Jean Gouzy, Jean Simon.

The material conditions for the negotiations left much to be desired as the delegates were gathered around a narrow, rectangular table without microphones. It was difficult to see the people who were talking when they were on your side of the table. Among the important questions discussed were the minimum wage (SMIG), the global increase in wages, and social security. The issues of public service and sliding scales would have to be negotiated later.

At 4:30 a.m. they separated into commissions to draft a compromise text. At about 7:30 the Prime Minister read the main clauses of the protocol: the minimum wage would rise from 2.22 francs to 3 francs an hour, salaries would increase by 10% (7% on 1 June and 3% in October), a 40 hour work week would become the norm, union freedom inside the workplace would be guaranteed, family allowances would be provided, worker training programs would be created, and so on. It was a big step forward. Notwithstanding these gains, nothing was proposed for the students. The proposals would amount to about fifteen billion francs being put into the consumer network, a colossal sum at the time. The delegations seemed satisfied, but would not sign, saying that the strike had been decided by the workers, so they must give their approval.

The Renault factory at Billancourt was used as a test case. The protocol was flatly rejected there. Ten million strikers in France felt the same way as Renault. They had been working hard for miserable wages too long, and so the continuation of the strike was agreed almost everywhere. Problems overlapped one another and perdured. Late in the morning electricity was cut off in different parts of the capital, ORTF refused to prepare the evening newscast at 8 p.m., and demonstrations continued in Paris and the provinces.

In an attempt to short-circuit the coalition between students and workers that it was strongly opposed to, the CGT organized twelve different demonstrations in Paris.

Charléty Stadium is located between the SNECMA, an aerospace engine manufacturer, and student housing. On Sunday, 26 May, when talks were being held at Rue Grenelle, Pierre Mendès France negotiated with Maurice Grimaud and Maurice Schuman to have a large gathering in an enclosed space. Charléty Stadium was decided on. Charles de Gaulle was against the assembly there, but his cabinet was strongly in favor of the idea and succeeded in persuading him. It was thought to be the best way of getting protestors off the street and into a closed space.

On 27 May a rendezvous was set for 5:30 p.m. at the Gobelins intersection. Ten thousand demonstrators were present at the beginning of the march, with Michel Rocard, Claude Bourdet, Pierre Mendès France up front, side by side with union leaders. It is difficult to estimate the number of people inside the stadium. Charléty has a capacity of 20,000, but there were a lot of people on the grass. In any case, the stadium was full. "The crowd seated on the bleachers was petty bourgeois, there were not many workers" (DAN 284). The atmosphere was jubilant after the demonstration the day before. Boys were running with girls on their shoulders and red and black flags were flapping in the wind.

Jacques Sauvageot spoke first at 7:15 to rally students. "Violence can be justified. Today, we don't think it's effective. The government, which has found some allies (laughter in the crowd), it must be said, is trying to divide students and workers. The Movement should be pushed to its ultimate consequences: the establishment of socialism." Next was Alain Geismar, who kept it short and sweet: "The primary duty of a revolutionary is to start the revolution."

André Barjonet, who had recently left the PCF and CGT, spoke next. "The situation we are in today is revolutionary. Everything is possible (applause). But we must organize ourselves and act very quickly . . . the revolution requires a flourishing of ideas" (DAN 285).

Aimé Halbeher, Deputy Secretary General at Renault Billancourt and an important figure in the occupation of the factory, took the microphone and said, "The CGT, CFDT and FO call upon workers to continue the strike." His laconic exhortation was punctuated by thunderous applause, after which he proceeded to enumerate union demands. What Halbeher did not know at the time, however, was that Georges Séguy had accepted all aspects of the compromise with the government.

Pierre Mendès France was in the audience and his name was called out, but he did not want to make a public statement. "We are here at a union meeting, it is not for me to speak," he declared. In fact, his presence at Charléty later cost him a seat in the National Assembly, because it labeled him a revolutionary. He lost the election in Grenoble to Jean-Marcel Jeanneney (DAN 285).

In the morning, Citroën, Sud-Aviation, Rhodiaceta and other smaller factories voted to continue the strike.

A feeling of panic had a strangle hold on the country. People were led to believe–television and the radio seemed to give that impression–that the negotiations at Rue Grenelle were the last chance for the government to resolve the social and economic crisis. If the rank and file refused to accept them, then nobody controlled anything anymore.

Many had an uncomfortable feeling that the CGT was playing some sort of game by only pretending to want to end the strike. Some, who were fed up with the social disorder, the piles of garbage in the street, the closed banks and gas stations, the long lines, and the empty supermarkets felt it was time to change governments. If Pompidou was incapable of restoring order, let Pierre Mendès France try. Maybe the revolutionaries would take over and wind up in the Élysée, with an anarchist leading the way. Barjonet did say that anything was possible.

Supermarkets and corner grocery stores were invaded by frantic housewives who grabbed what they could from the shelves and began hoarding food. Dark memories of Paris during the occupation were haunting people's minds, when the Nazis took everything. Parisian families with a house in the country left the city, if they could siphon enough gasoline from someone else's car. It was often said that during the German Occupation the only people not to go hungry were the peasants in the provinces, people living in the country and in small villages where there was less control. There was some truth to that.

The political situation in France, already torrid, was heating up even more, and the different political parties were hoping to profit from the situation. The CGT largely controlled the strike and did not like to see militant students going to the factories and provoking the CRS. The PCF did not trust the students either, and had criticized them on numerous occasions, especially Daniel Cohn-Bendit. François Mitterrand and Pierre Mendès France had big ambitions and were seeking an opportunity to move up the political ladder. The communists could not govern alone, they needed allies. That is where the Federation of the Democratic and Socialist

Left (FGDS) came in. There was Mollet, Billères and Mitterrand. But François Mitterrand had a strong will and a mind of his own; he was far too independent for many in the PCF. By the same token, Mitterrand needed the communists, too. Waldeck Rochet, General Secretary from 1964 to 1972, sent a public letter to Mitterrand proposing a popular and democratic union with the participation of communists and a minimum program. He chose to send a public letter because he did not trust the leader of the Federation of the Democratic and Socialist Left (FGDS).

The PCF had enormous power in 1968 and strong ties with the Soviet Union. For that reason it scared many, and not just political conservatives. So Mitterrand could not openly endorse communist proposals, because it could mean the end of his political career. He advocated a rebalancing of the political left, which meant he favored reform, liberalism and democratic principles, as opposed to the methods and ideology of Stalin and the USSR (JOF 296).

Radical students had contacted Mendès France, the former president of the Council, several times. Marc Heurgon, political adviser for Jacques Sauvageot, was one of the mainstays of the new coalition. Centrists had also supported Mendès France. With these things in mind, Mitterrand felt the pressure and knew he needed to act quickly, or he would be left holding the bag. But it was a big gamble at the same time, because it could arouse antagonism.

Pierre Mendès France had seen Alain Geismar a few times as well, and they were on friendly terms, even if they were often at odds. For the young radicals, Mendès France might be the man they were looking for, since he could hold things together during the transition period. Later, they could get rid of him if he did not work out the way they wanted.

A casual meeting was set up at Marcel-Francis Kahn's

residence. There were representatives from the CFDT, SNE-sup, and Sauvageot for UNEF. The purpose was to find a solution to the crisis. "They're giving us gadgets. The gadget Mitterrand, the gadget Mendès. The population does not need another government, what it needs is real power inside the workplace," said Sauvageot. Mendès France found the discussions verbose, short-sighted and unrealistic.

"Everything is falling apart. The French no longer have the feeling they are being represented by their representatives. The situation is revolutionary. To find a way out, we must form a government made up of all the leftists, including communists and various allied groups," proposed Mendès France (JOF 298).

Sauvageot and the students flatly rejected this plan. "The only service you can render the nation is to say publicly that the situation is revolutionary," said the leader of UNEF. But that would have been political suicide for Mendès France.

The meeting ended, like so many others, with nothing being decided. Marcel Gonin summarized the ambiguity of student demands when he said, "You're in favor of forcing Mendès France to accept authority, and all in favor of making the task impossible for him" (JOF 299).

On 28 May, François Mitterrand organized a press conference at the Continental Hotel at 11 a.m. Mitterrand represented the traditional left in politics, the parliamentary left, which was worlds apart from the student left of Sauvageot. His announcement was, to say the least, an attack against the government and Gaullism.

"In France, ever since 3 May 1968, there has been no government, and what is taking its place does not even have a semblance of power," he began. Mitterrand made two assertions: 1) Republicans will vote "no" on the 16 June referendum-plebiscite, 2) general de Gaulle's departure, before or after 16 June, will naturally result in the departure of the Prime Minister and his government (JOF 303).

In light of his hypotheses, Mitterrand suggested that a provisional government should be set up to manage the country's affairs. It would be made up of ten persons, with no one debarred and without attempts at political balancing. Its goal would be to get the country working again by negotiating with students and workers to respond to the many valid demands of different social and professional groups; and, finally, to organize the necessary conditions for the next presidential election.

"If necessary, I will assume the responsibility of forming the provisional government, but others besides myself can legitimately assume this responsibility. I'm thinking of Pierre Mendès France" (JOF 303-4). With regards to the presidential election he added: "Because the referendum is in eighteen days, and because we are fighting the same combat, I'm announcing my candidature [for president]."

Mitterrand's speech was filmed by the ORTF, making him appear to be a seditious revolutionary, according to Laurent Joffrin. Mitterrand would often be criticized for his audacious declarations.

Gaston Monnerville, president of the Senate, was outraged by the announcement, and was sure the opposition had lost thousands of votes, if not millions, because of Mitterrand's rashness. But then again, maybe his declaration was not as rash as that. In the fervor of Charléty, he was exercising his role as president of the FGDS. De Gaulle's departure from the government was not a wild fancy. But when he evoked the plan to set up a "managing government," he was overstepping his authority and misinforming the public.

The French Constitution does not provide for anything of the kind. If a French president resigned, the official government, in this case George Pompidou's government, remained in power. It was the legitimate government according to the Constitution. Gaston Monnerville, as president of the Senate, could not designate another one, unless the Prime Minister resigned. Mitterrand said it would be "natural," but that was a subjective analysis. It was certainly not compulsory. But the political left believed, or wanted to believe, that the nationwide strikes and demonstrations would force Georges Pompidou out of Matignon.

Waldeck Rochet, General Secretary of the PCF, along with the rest of the party, did not at all approve of Mitterrand's announcement which he saw as opportunistic and self-indulgent. In response the PCF published a virulent communiqué saying there could not be any social programs without the participation of the communist party. Neither could there be socialism in France without the active participation of the communists. Moreover, the PCF said it did not intend to let other politicians substitute themselves for the legitimate government in office if they were incapable of satisfying the people's demands. Nor did the PCF intend to let a regime take power that had pledged its allegiance to the American government. Of course the PCF supported the USSR, and the Cold War was at its height in 1968.

The CGT called for a massive demonstration on 29 May 1968, and the route of the procession would not be too far from City Hall and the Élysée Palace. Were the communists going to attempt a power play? Pompidou did not think so, but he was cautious enough to have the country's reservists ready just in case. Squadrons of the gendarmerie in Satory were on alert. In Castres and Carcasonne, paratroopers were on alert as well as troops in Toulon, Monthléry and Maisons-Lafitte. But in all truth, neither Grimaud, Fouchet nor Messmer were willing to use the army in such a turbulent and uncertain context. It was probably safe to say that apart from a few close friends to general de Gaulle, the army did not want to get mixed up in a political affair, if it could avoid it.

To counter the march, Pompidou gave his approval for a Gaullist demonstration, scheduled for 30 May in the afternoon. Pierre-Charles Krieg was attributed with that brainstorm.

On 27 May the project for the referendum was passed during the Council of Ministers. The text provided for reforming higher education, business and the administrative regions of France. Gaullists believed the text would put the country at the avant-garde of social and economic progress, between capitalism and socialism. Pompidou was rightfully concerned about the logistics and the practical aspects of the election, feeling it would be difficult to implement in a nation paralyzed by strikes. The public, for its part, could not imagine strikers deliberately sabotaging a democratic election. But things were unpredictable in May-June 1968.

Pompidou's strategy worked. Student violence on 24 May changed public opinion; that and the continuation of the strike. Communications were being disrupted and even the Ministry of the Interior encountered problems in Paris and the provinces because the PTT was partially on strike. The rejection of the Grenelle protocol by the rank and file of Billancourt shattered any hope of an end to labor turmoil. The most significant social and economic concessions since World War Two solved nothing.

The Sorbonne, still occupied by students on 28 May, held an assembly every evening. Daniel Cohn-Bendit managed to sneak back to Paris and went to his favorite hangout to rally the troops. With his dyed hair and dark glasses nobody recognized him, but after saying a few words he was met with a resounding ovation. It was like Ulysses returning to his kingdom of Ithaca disguised as a beggar. The color of his hair had changed but not his impetuous temperament. The government, he said, must be forced to resign. "I was deported under the pretext that I had disturbed the public order. Therefore I ask that those who disturbed the public order by bringing the police into the Sorbonne and the Latin Quarter, the Provost and the Minister of the Interior, be deported." Furthermore, he was not "a foreign agent," but was part of an international revolution (KER 97). Somebody informed a local radio station and they broke the news. Dany was always newsworthy.

At the Élysée Palace Charles de Gaulle was in a gloomy mood. He did not know what to do to get the country back to work and back in the classroom. France was in chaos, paralyzed by the national strikes. And his Prime Minister and cabinet were not doing what he wanted them to do, in particular concerning the reopening of the Sorbonne. Gaullist cohesion seemed to be falling apart and some members of the National Assembly felt it was time for the General to pack his bags and return to the Boisserie, which was what he was about to do.

On the 29th of May, Charles de Gaulle arrived in his office at about 9 a.m., which was earlier than usual. He saw Xavier de la Chevalerie, director of his cabinet, told him he was tired and that he was going to Colombey-les-Deux-Églises. He would leave a message for Pompidou saying that the Council of Ministers was postponed until the next day at 3 p.m. De Gaulle's son-in-law, Alain de Boissieu, had a short conversation with his father-in-law, though it is not clear exactly when that was. "The French are like calves, and calves are meant to be eaten. So what do I do with the calf's head? I'd be better off to go back home and write my memoirs," declared de Gaulle. De Boissieu, who was highly critical of what the government had been doing over the past two weeks, stood at attention and addressed his father-in-law, who also stood at attention. "The army is loyal. The army is waiting for its orders, and it will no longer accept being made to look ridiculous."

De Gaulle was not sleeping well and needed to break with the routine of Paris to be able to think clearly. With his wife and family, he left the Élysée very discreetly by the "grille du coq," a large iron gate that was used on special occasions. At 11:45 a.m. two "Allouettes" (large helicopters) were waiting to take off. Once the passengers were aboard they headed east. At 12:50 they stopped to refuel at Saint-Dizier before landing at Baden-Baden in West Germany. Nobody knew where de Gaulle was at this time, his disappearance was a mystery, even for the government.

Everything has fouled up, the communists have blocked everything, he told general Jacques Massu, who quickly noticed that de Gaulle was not his normal self. Massu later said he gave words of encouragement to the French president, telling him he did not have the right to drop everything. Even if he was the target of another assassination attempt, it would be better for his image to continue fighting.

At 4:30 p.m. de Gaulle and his family took the helicopters to Colombey-les-Deux-Églises and arrived at about 6 p.m. They were driven to the family estate, the Boisserie, in a police car. Once at home, he went for a walk in his spacious park.

In Paris, the next day, there was a demonstration organized by the CGT at the Bastille. De Gaulle called Bernard Tricot, General Secretary of the Élysée. A good night's sleep seemed to have changed everything. Naturally, his disappearance was a difficult test for the government of Georges Pompidou. "I made an agreement with my ulterior motives," de Gaulle said, meaning that he was ready to take control of the situation.

An atmosphere of uncertainly lingered in the streets of Paris. What would happen if violence broke out again? Would there be military intervention? De Gaulle and his government wanted to avoid that if possible.

On 30 May at 11:05, de Gaulle took a helicopter in Colombey back to Paris. He arrived at the Élysée at 12:25 p.m. The president was resolute. He knew what to do. His collaborators were quick to notice how determined he was. "He was wearing his 1940 boots," someone remarked.

There are different theories about what was going through the General's mind. For Jacques Massu and Georges Pompidou, Charles de Gaulle suffered a kind of depression. He was discouraged and frustrated by the situation in the country he was devoted to. Moreover, he was not sleeping well, and that alone was capable of causing discouragement and depression. When de Gaulle and his family arrived in Baden-Baden, arrangements were made for a prolonged stay. They had packed many more suitcases than usual, also suggesting an extended stay.

Others–who constitute the majority of authors–reject Massu and Pompidou's interpretation, and see the "disappearance" as a sort of strategy, the strategy of surprise. According to these authors de Gaulle knew that the referendum would fail. In June he told Michel Droit that he was tempted to withdraw from politics. In his speech on the radio on 30 May, he said he had envisioned "every possibility."

Charles de Gaulle was the incarnation of his country's destiny. He had been present during its most difficult moments: the war in Algeria, the Cold War and the threat of atomic weapons, the departure from OTAN, the European Union, and the post-war industrial boom. For many, he was and always would be a military general; with his back to the wall, he would be weighing his opponent's capacities in order to prepare a counterattack. Indeed, it could be said that there were two men in Charles de Gaulle: the private and the public. The private man had simple tastes and delighted in simple pleasures. The public man was disciplined, devoted to his country, and a terrible loser.

Georges Pompidou was generous with the student movement, but his generosity was probably interpreted as a sign of weakness by the political left that saw it as a signal to step on the accelerator and up the ante. On 24 May the time was not right to slow down the Movement, but on 30 May, the public was afraid of the future, and they wanted to get ready for their summer vacation.

The dilemma for the opposition at this time was to find a way to get Pierre Mendès France, who looked exhausted physically, and the communists to agree to some sort of cohabitation.

General de Gaulle told Jacques Foccart, the General Secretary for the Community, what he was going to say. Foccart informed him when the demonstration was scheduled to begin, so de Gaulle decided to give his speech after the Council of Ministers (DAN 320).

At 2:30 p.m. on 30 May during the Council of Ministers, Georges Pompidou was going to resign because the president had disappeared for a day without telling him why. De Gaulle refused to accept his resignation. He smiled and simply said their fates were inextricably tied together. Then he read his speech to the Prime Minister. The speech was fine, said Pompidou, but he had forgotten to say he was going to dissolve the National Assembly. Some maintain that the dissolution of the Assembly was Pompidou's idea. He handed Pompidou the letter he had written for Gaston Monnerville, president of the Senate–Article 12 of the Constitution required his knowledge of the dissolution.

Monnerville, born in Cayenne in French Guiana and grandson of a former slave, hated de Gaulle and hoped he would resign. He had met with several politicians from different parties and told a prefect whom he knew intimately that soon he would take control. One can only surmise what would have happened if Charles de Gaulle had resigned then, before the referendum. What is certain, however, is that different groups sought to gain control of the Republic.

After the Council of Ministers at 4:30 p.m., de Gaulle gave his speech on the radio, fearing perhaps that the ORTF and the striking technicians might decide to cut his broadcast short, but also because he was tired. Maybe, too, because the radio was accessible to everyone–not all families had a television in 1968. The sound alone was broadcast on television. But to be honest, Charles de Gaulle was more effective on the radio than on TV. De Gaulle seemed cramped and too old-fashioned on the little screen, with his emphatic gestures and awkward pauses. His discourse was more powerful on the radio, where his voice echoed on the airwaves like an old friend from the past, perhaps vaguely evoking Radio Londres, used by de Gaulle and the Free French during World War Two.

De Gaulle's text was short and to the point, the tone was emphatic and the diction denoted resolve. "I am not resigning," he affirmed, as a sort of exordium for what was to follow. Nor would he change Pompidou, his well-read professor, "whose merit, resistance and loyalty deserve everyone's praise." He was dissolving the National Assembly, he announced with a sort of satisfaction. The referendum, which he chose because it was "the only acceptable way, that of democracy," would give voters the chance to reform the economy and the university system. It would take place at a later date because the present situation made it impossible to hold. The legislative election would be organized according to the procedure described in the Constitution, unless, of course, "some were intending to gag the country by preventing citizens from expressing themselves while they prevent them from living, the same way they prevent students from studying, teachers from teaching, and workers from working. The methods employed are intimidation, intoxication and tyranny used by well-established groups, and a political party that is a totalitarian organization." If that force was maintained, he would have to use other means, provided for by the Constitution, in order to hold the Republic together. "France is in fact threatened by a dictatorship," he asserted. Some were attempting to force the country to submit, because of national despair, to "totalitarian communism." But, of course, that power would be disguised with a false appearance.

By using the fearsome words "dictatorship and totalitarian communism," he alluded to the PCF and CGT directly, and the USSR indirectly. De Gaulle, like Pompidou, decided to use fear to move his audience, warning his listeners that the danger was not imaginary but very real, and involved the ostensible threat of communist subversion to install a totalitarian regime. France could recognize, then, who its real enemies were: strikers that prevent students from studying, teachers from teaching and workers from working. Without naming names, everyone got the picture when he referred to "politicians ready for the scrap heap," in other words Mendès France and Mitterrand. Mentioning Article 16 of the

Constitution that gave all power to the executive was a thinly disguised warning: if the general strike continued, if the elections were sabotaged by the opposition, he could use that Article to restore order; perhaps even call out the army to break the strike.

In the Bourbon Palace where the National Assembly meets, the ambiance was euphoric, and the allocution was punctuated by applause and cheers, with a hearty rendition of the Marseillaise sung to conclude. De Gaulle's speech sent shockwaves throughout the Hexagon.

At the Sorbonne the speech was met with boos and jeers and people calling for a civil war. Rumor had it that the tanks were already on their way to encircle university campuses.

The political left was outraged. François Mitterrand counterattacked by telling journalists that the voice they heard on the radio was that of a "dictatorship," and that what the president said was nothing less than "an act of war." The PCF reiterated that idea by saying it was "a true declaration of war." But, in fact, war had already been declared by the Movement.

"Students were the ones who protested. And what does de Gaulle offer to solve our problems? Elections, even though most of us cannot vote," protested 22 March.

Words can be mightier than swords, and de Gaulle found the words he had been looking for to end the Movement. The population was not ready for a civil war, and reform was in the offing. By way of apotheosis, Jacques Chaban-Delmas read a short message from the Élysée:

"Mr. President,

I am honored to inform you that in virtue of Article 12 of the Constitution, and after having consulted with the personalities provided for by this article, I have decided to proceed with the dissolution of the National Assembly."

A relatively small crowd was expected for the demonstration in support of de Gaulle: 50,000 at the most. It proved to be larger than Woodstock, or at least as large.

The Tricolor was conspicuous. The crowd was made up of everyday people who had had their fill of burned automobiles, violence in the street, and insults thrown at a man who defended the Republic against totalitarianism.

Banderoles streaming in the wind expressed the deeper feelings of the crowd: "De Gaulle is not alone," "Communism will not wash." The procession chanted slogans such as "Mitterrand charlatan," "Cohn-Bendit to Berlin," or "Cohn-Bendit to Dachau." The march of support ended at around 9 p.m. at the flame of the Unknown Soldier.

At 9 p.m., after the demonstration, Georges Pompidou, in agreement with Olivier Guichard, Minister of Industry, gave the order to supply gas stations the next day. The long weekend of the Pentecost was about to begin, and if Parisians could get away for three days to forget their troubles, they would be a lot happier. Miraculously, like the Holy Spirit descending upon the disciples, gas stations were resupplied on Friday morning, 31 May.

June

May ended with de Gaulle's allocution on the thirtieth and the march in support of him. The tide had turned decisively in favor of the government and the Gaullists, who now had the momentum and the support of public opinion. June 68 would not be like May 68. The three day break because of the Pentecost brought about a change of attitudes. The student movement, on the other hand, seemed winded and stale. The gestures and slogans had become repetitive. A strategy for change cannot be based on barricades and cobblestones. Those who believed in the Republic could not identify with the black flags and the red flags. So where could students go from there? Groups that are advocating revolution have limited options, and the choices of revolutionary groups will, by definition, be extreme. The Weather Underground in the United States declared war on the government, but by doing so they ran blindly into a dead-end street. Blowing things up is not a long-term strategy, unless your ultimate goal is absolute destruction.

Of course, not everyone in the student movement was a wannabe revolutionary. At least some believed in Pierre Mendès France, but the revolutionaries did not because Mendès France was a realist and not a revolutionary.

The student movement, as is often the case, lacked a coherent plan for achieving long-term goals. This was probably so because when people stopped being students, they moved on to other things, like raising a family and working full time. Sporadic attempts at regrouping failed. A case in point was the Revolutionary Movement with André Barjonet, a disillusioned militant who had left both the PCF and the CGT. He expressed his ideas about May 1968 in *La Révolution trahie*, published in 1968.

An attempt at coordination by Jean-Pierre Vigier, a physician who broke with the PCF, also failed. He assumed the fulltime responsibilities of director of the journal *Action*, mouthpiece of leftist groups such as UNEF, SNE-sup, 22 March, and CAL. The endeavor to coordinate Local Action Committees fizzled out because the various factions could not agree on anything substantial. Maoists refused to abandon control of the Action Committees and Daniel Cohn-Bendit, being opposed to direction from the top of the pyramid, advocated grass roots discussions (DAN 332). It had to be direct democracy or nothing. This attempt at coordination was probably doomed to failure since the different factions had divergent views on many issues including workers' councils and the kinds of militancy that were acceptable.

Student leaders must have been aware at this point that they had let their chance slip away and that they were on a fool's errand, though attempts were made to spark radical enthusiasm.

On the first of June, UNEF organized a march with the theme "Elections-Treason." About 15,000 people participated; students said there were more than twice that many. Persons outside the movement may have found the theme paradoxical, but the point was that many students could not vote because you had to be twenty-one. The voting age would be lowered in 1974 to eighteen.

Dany was still in town and on Saturday evening in the large lecture hall at the Sorbonne he raged against workers returning to work (DAN 332). Alain Geismar reiterated that motif two days later. On Tuesday, 4 June, Youths United for Gaullism reportedly assembled 25,000 demonstrators in a march that went from Trocadero to Montparnasse Station.

Negotiations between employees and employers had been at a standstill ever since the abortive attempt to conclude at Grenelle, but some discussions were resumed during the long weekend of the Pentecost, and agreements were reached in small and medium-size businesses, notably in the textile industry. It seemed easier for employers to increase wages than to decrease working hours. An agreement was signed at EDF, but a consensus was more difficult to reach in department stores.

One by one the strikes ended, with the civil servants returning to work first, then on 5 June the SNCF, PTT and the state owned public transit in Paris (RATP) went back to work. On 6 June the FEN lifted the strike order and children returned to school.

On 4 June 1968, police invaded Flins where a picket line was supposed to prevent the return to work. Strikers were removed but the strike continued until 15 June. Renault began production again on 17 June, Citroën on 24 June, Usinor-Dunkerque on 26 June. But by 19 June there were only 150,000 strikers in France (DAN 333).

If June was marked by a change in the government's attitude, there was probably a change in the way police dealt with strikers, too. There were four deaths in June. Gilles Tautin drowned in the Seine River near Meulan on 10 June when he tried to get away from the CRS (IA 83-84). News of his death spread quickly and several thousand students gathered in Saint-Michel Boulevard to shout their outrage. There were violent confrontations with the police all night long and barricades were constructed (GOF 96-97). On 15 June five thousand people marched in silence to honor the memory of Gilles Tautin, seventeen, buried that day at the Batignolles cemetery.

Pierre Beylot, employed at Peugeot, was shot by the CRS with a 9mm bullet. Henri Blanchet fell off a wall and died when a grenade exploded. There were three deaths in two days, and five deaths in all: two students, two workers, and one policeman (GOF 96). Maurice Grimaud added commander Journiac of the CRS to the list. He was hit in the head by a cobblestone during the riots of 10-11 May, in Rue Gay-Lussac.

On 12 June, the government increased its tempo of censure by imposing restrictions on demonstrations: 1) no demonstrations were allowed during the electoral campaign, 2) eleven leftwing organizations including JCR, FER, 22 March and UJCML were declared illegal, 3) foreigners who took part in the leftwing demonstrations were deported. Daniel Cohn-Bendit returned to Germany rather than run the risk of being arrested and imprisoned.

On Friday, 14 June at 9 a.m. police surrounded the Odéon. Plainclothes policemen entered the theater and gave an ultimatum to the persons squatting there. "Those that want to leave must leave now. They will be free to go if they evacuate the building without weapons and without acts of hostility" (DAN 336). About one hundred persons left the theater without incident.

On Saturday, 16 June, after a few useless discussions, the police "liberated" the Sorbonne in much the same manner as the Odéon had been "liberated." The "Katangais" had been previously thrown out by students.

After the first round of elections, which was highly favorable to Gaullists, the General addressed the public in a televised allocution the day before the second round to ask voters to ensure him a majority in the National Assembly. This would have three principle objectives: guarantee the unity of the nation, overcome the severe handicap caused by the May crisis, and empower the government to initiate social reform to safeguard human dignity. During the speech, he said the nation was scandalized by student anarchists that sought to pull the Republic into the abyss, and also by the general strike that paralyzed the country. As president, he had addressed the nation, and the nation responded. The national instinct had finally been resuscitated. France, he affirmed, had only been saved from disaster by a strong government. Renewed prosperity was possible if the nation was united and productive. Active participation by everyone, whether in industry or higher education, must become the guiding rule. The destiny of France was at stake.

Gaullists and conservatives won a landslide victory in the legislative elections held on 23 and 30 June. As a result of these elections, the presidential majority controlled the National Assembly with 394 seats: The Union for the Defense of the Republic (UDR), created by the Gaullists, had 294 seats and Independent Republicans (RI) had 64. The political left had only 91 seats: the PCF had 34 and the Federation of the Democratic and Socialist Left (FGDS) 57. The June election can be interpreted as a public condemnation of the riots and strikes of May 68, and approbation of Georges Pompidou and the Gaullists.

The constitutional referendum announced by president de Gaulle, which had been postponed several times, was finally held on 27 April 1969. It was rejected by the population: 52.41% voted no, or 12,007,102 voters; 47.59% voted yes, or 10,901,753 voters. There was 19.87% abstention, with 5,680,856 people, the lowest of the previous referendums. There were a significant number of blank votes with 635,678.

After the election results were known, Charles de Gaulle

simply said, "I cease my functions as president of the Republic. This decision takes effect today at noon."

It was a goodbye without saying goodbye. Two weeks later he would appear in Ireland with his wife Yvonne. He seemed older, walked with a cane and a stoop. Charles de Gaulle would have about eighteen months of retirement.

Violence and Brutality

French law provides for the prosecution of persons who willingly commit violent acts against other persons: Article 309 of the Penal Code (Ord. ns 58-1297 of 23-12-8, art.). "Any individual who voluntarily causes harm, commits assault or assault with a deadly weapon, or as a result of this physical violence the victim is sick or incapacitated for more than 8 days, will be punished by 2 months to 5 years in prison and fined 50,000 to a million francs." Article 186 states that if civil servants or government officers physically abuse persons without a legitimate motive, the law provides for their punishment according to the nature of their offense. Article 198 states that it is a crime for civil servants or government officers to take part in other crimes or offenses that they were called upon to watch over or to repress.

With regards to detention and identity checks, Article 61, paragraph 2 states that during a "criminal search," persons are required to disclose their identity. The text does not say how long it should take to accomplish this. Article 66 of the Constitution of 4 October 1958, states that "no one can be arbitrarily detained." It follows, therefore, that verifications of identity, as interpreted within the framework of the Constitution, should not be unduly long, nor should it deprive persons of their liberty.

One of the biggest scandals of May 1968 was about police beating wounded or innocent persons and preventing medical assistance to the injured. Numerous testimonies show that the forces of law and order physically prevented doctors and first aid attendants from taking care of the wounded. Mr. Blum, a lawyer, asked the assistant director of police headquarters, Mr. Grosperrin, if he knew how many students had been wounded during the demonstration on Friday, 3 May. He replied by saying: "They didn't try to make themselves known to the police, and . . . it's a good thing for them they didn't" (IA 113).

The following testimonies were given by persons who witnessed violence and brutality during the events of May-June 1968. They were taken from two texts written by UNEF and SNE-sup, published in 1968, only a few months after the demonstrations. The first book is entitled *Le Livre noir des journées de mai*, the second *Ils accusent*. More than 600 testimonies were gathered in just two months for the second, and special care was taken to be sure of their authenticity. The identity of the witnesses, detailed information with regards to the time, place, date and reported facts were systematically asked for and noted. On the other hand, it would be impossible to verify the exactitude of all the claims. From the beginning, hundreds of persons were scandalized by the official versions of events and sought to report the truth about what really happened. As one reads through these testimonies basic patterns of behavior become apparent.

Testimony 504: On the night of 10-11 May, at the corner of Rue Gay-Lussac, a hospital doctor saw police refusing to evacuate wounded persons and would even grab them from first aid attendants and beat them with their billy clubs, then take them away in a police car. Police would also require the identity of wounded persons before they could be evacuated (IA 113-14). This odious behavior prompted the medical doctor to publish a communiqué the next day with several of his colleagues. The same doctor saw a man and woman attacked with savage violence by five CRS at the corner of Saint-Michel Boulevard and the Rue de l'École de Médecine. First they were viciously clubbed, then kicked in the chest and abdomen when they were on the ground. They were dragged half conscious to a police car without permitting medical services to take care of them.

Testimony 373: On 24-25 May, in Ledru-Rollin Avenue, police or CRS prevented a medical doctor from examining a prisoner they were holding in a car, and who was said to be wounded. The prisoner, they claimed, was being submitted to a simple interrogation. Another doctor said that as soon as their backs were turned they heard screaming from the police car (IA 114).

Not all first aid workers were brave enough to oppose the police to do their job and assist wounded persons. On Sébastopol Boulevard members of the Red Cross refused to go near groups of demonstrators because their organization told them to obey police instructions, and they were prevented from crossing police barricades. When they were carrying a stretcher to get wounded persons, they were chased by the police who wanted to take it away. Near Ledru-Rollin Avenue, a man was being beaten by the CRS or police with their clubs. The medical attendants saved the man by taking him away from the police.

First aid workers usually had good reasons if they hesitated from shielding the wounded from the forces of law and order. They were not just confronted with refusals but with threats, verbal abuse and in some cases arrests and beatings. Many medical workers were unable to prevent the CRS and police from beating a wounded person.

Testimony 361: On 25 May at 1 a.m. these witnesses heard grenades, so they went downstairs to open the doors of the building. About 30 demonstrators were running away from a large number of CRS. Behind them were ten police vans. After they ran away, a car that was coming from the

Place de la République and moving slowly was stopped by the CRS at the corner of Beaumarchais Boulevard and the Rue Saint-Gilles. The driver was pulled out of the car and beaten to the ground. He was wounded. A Red Cross car came and tried to administer first aid to this person, but the CRS would not let them and took the driver away (IA 115).

The CRS entered apartment buildings, and when that was not possible, they relied on more primitive means. This witness says they broke a window and threw a teargas grenade inside, thereby forcing the occupants to go downstairs into the courtyard where they were beaten against the walls and undressed by the CRS. A young girl was thus forced to come out into the street almost naked, and was pushed from one cop to the next, then beaten like the other injured persons. For 150 meters she was forced to exhibit herself to everyone in the neighborhood when she was taken from the Rue Royer-Collard to the Rue des Fossés-Saint-Jacques and the waiting police van where a reporter who had previously been arrested gave her his shirt (LN 74).

Another witness saw a similar incident. A representative of the forces of law and order threw a rock through a window of the second floor, and two grenades were thrown inside, forcing the occupants of the studio to come out. Eight to ten people, including a young girl, were forced to stand in front of a wall of the courtyard, where a "genuine massacre" took place. The group of youths was beaten nonstop for ten minutes. The clothing of the young girl was violently ripped off her: "her red dress, her brassiere, and half of her petticoat." One of the cops yelled, "You slut, we're going to make you parade naked through the streets of Paris" (LN 75).

A physician affirms that he too saw the CRS shoot grenades into apartments, in this case in the Rue Pierre-et-

Marie-Curie (LN 76). Numerous other witnesses testify to the CRS shooting or throwing grenades into windows or at balconies at 69 Saint-Michel Boulevard and the first few houses of the Rue Royer-Collard, although the persons who were targeted were merely spectators of the violence in the streets below (LN 83). Such was also the case in Rue Gay-Lussac, where a store owner was forced to close shop indefinitely because "teargas grenades were thrown into the hallway and into the store" (LN 83).

Numerous testimonies state that the forces of law and order brutalized many persons who were very seriously wounded.

Testimony 440: On 24-25 May on Saint-Michel Boulevard during the last charge of the CRS, a wounded man sought shelter in a hallway, at 53 Saint-Michel Boulevard. He was pursued by several CRS who pummeled him with their nightsticks when they caught him. Another CRS threw a teargas grenade into the corridor. Nurses who arrived on the scene tried to help the man in the hallway, but there was so much gas there they came right back out to administer first aid to themselves. Then other nurses arrived who had gasmasks and were able to assist the wounded man. They said that he looked like a "puppet with dislocated limbs." Upon leaving the building they found two teargas canisters in the hallway (IA 115).

Testimony 472: On Wednesday, 13 June 1968, at 1:30 a.m. at the Barbès-Rochechouart metro station, after the charge of CRS from the Bouches-du-Rhône, a demonstrator fell down about one hundred meters from the police vans. A medical worker went to help the person, but two CRS grabbed him and started taking him towards their van. Suddenly, the two CRS aggressively pushed the wounded person into the arms of the medical worker who helped him to move towards the medical vehicles. About 20 CRS then surrounded the vehicle and wanted to take the person back. The first aid worker opposed the CRS who immediately raised their nightsticks in a threatening manner. One CRS hit the medical worker in the chest with his rifle butt, and a person who tried to help his colleague was hit in the shoulder. At that point the CRS took the wounded man to the van and beat him up (IA 115).

Testimony 793: On 13 July 1968, at midnight, in Saint-Michel Boulevard the CRS shot teargas grenades for no apparent reason. A farmer was shot with one in the head and was lying unconscious in the street for two hours. Police rescue teams refused to take him to the hospital and said, "We're here to kick ass, not to take care of the wounded" (IA 116).

Testimony 397: This incident occurred on 25 May 1968, at 4 a.m. in Rue Danton. A volunteer first aid attendant saw a young demonstrator caught between two groups of CRS who beat him up with unprecedented savagery. The youth was bleeding profusely from the face. When the first aid worker tried to assist the injured person, a motorcycle cop threatened him with a cobblestone and said, "Get out of here."

Testimony 759: This occurred on Saint-Michel Boulevard, 5 May. A witness saw two police officers who had just taken a wounded prisoner. One of the cops pushed him forward as he strangled him with his nightstick, while the other cop hit him in the face with his club. The prisoner's forehead had an open wound, and his face was covered with blood. His nose was probably broken and maybe his skull, too. He lost consciousness. A Red Cross worker wearing the official uniform of the organization tried to help the unconscious victim, but was threatened by the police. One policeman brandished his billy club in intimidation, and so the nurse was forced to leave (IA 116).

Some questions have been raised concerning the nature of certain groups of police. A medical doctor testified concerning the "savage beating" he witnessed on 6 May, at about 6 p.m. in Saint-Michel Boulevard, a few meters from Rue Saint-Séverin (LN 26). A young man with long hair was "savagely beaten up for no apparent reason" by men wearing khaki uniforms. The confrontations between police and students at the barricades were happening elsewhere, in Saint-Germain Boulevard. The young man was walking along the sidewalk, on the odd-numbered side of the street. The "police" were not wearing navy blue uniforms; they had a military aspect. It was the first time the doctor had seen "police" wearing that kind of uniform. The men came out of a police van that had just stopped in front of the café on the corner. They beat the young man on the head with their nightsticks, and the noise of the sticks hitting his skull was horrible. When they finished beating him up, they went back to their van without worrying about what the passersby thought or did. The doctor helped the youth to his feet and noticed a tuft of hair torn off.

The following testimony was given by a volunteer nurse (LN 81). "When Europe 1 (a radio station) issued a plea for medicine, we drove to Rue François I to pick it up. When we were about to leave, we were surrounded by police and CRS who threw the medicine on the pavement."

One thing that was much discussed in the newspapers was the burning of cars in the street. Who was responsible, the demonstrators or the police? The following testimonies give information about that controversy.

Rue Royer-Collard is a short street that goes from the Rue Gay-Lussac to Saint-Michel Boulevard. There were three cars there. During the first charge by the CRS, the witness saw the forces of law and order burn these cars. "As far as I know, it was the first known case of burned cars" (LN 84).

On Saturday at about 4:30 a.m. in the Rue ULM, the witness saw a car set on fire there by a grenade that was thrown by the police (LN 84).

Persons saw the CRS vans coming down Saint-Michel Boulevard. When they stopped, several CRS got out of the vehicles with grayish-white cases, from which they took projectiles which they shot with rifles or small, very light "canons." The barricades, made of cars and stones, were set on fire as soon as the projectiles exploded on them. The same thing occurred in the Rue Royer-Collard. When the projectiles hit the barricades with a greenish-white light, the barricade burst into flames. They set the cars on fire very quickly (LN 84).

On Saturday, 11 May at 3:30 a.m., a university Professor was at 11 Rue Pierre-et-Marie-Curie in the courtyard of the scientific institutes (LN 77). Only the Henri-Poincaré Institute was open and was being used as a first aid station. The professor saw a group of police come running into the courtyard, chasing people with their billy clubs. An Assistant Professor from the faculty of science was standing in front of the first aid station. When he saw the police he yelled at them: "This is a first aid station." One of the policemen answered back, "We don't give a damn about your first aid station" and hit the Assistant Professor with his club. He was about to hit him again when a Professor at the Sorbonne grabbed him by the arm and said: "I am a Professor at the Sorbonne. This is part of the university; you have no business being here, leave immediately." After a few seconds of hesitation, a policeman who must have been a high-ranking officer said to them: "Alright. Back up! But close your gates."

According to numerous testimonies, it was not at all uncommon for the CRS and police to attack first aid workers.

Testimony 782: A first aid worker on 11-12 June at between four and five in the morning was going back to the Sorbonne infirmary by taking the Rue Saint-Jacques. When he got there he turned around and saw a guy on the sidewalk with a bloody neck. The attendant put the man on his back and started to carry him. Some CRS, enraged because they did not get the guy first, threw several offensive grenades–maybe as many as fifteen–into the entrance of the infirmary. The attendant was hit in the eye with a grenade. ("The witness's eye "exploded.") The cops refused to let him be evacuated, so he waited half an hour before being taken to Cochin Hospital (IA 117).

Testimony 769: On 25 May an assistant film director saw a CRS officer knock a student out with a cobblestone while he was trying to close the iron gate of the Sorbonne. A few minutes later, three or four CRS used their clubs to severely beat a demonstrator. A photographer wearing a cap with the word "Press" on it took a picture of the group of cops and the student lying on the ground. The police promptly left the beaten student and went after the photographer, knocked off his cap, grabbed his camera and knocked him out, leaving him lying on the ground. First aid attendants wearing white smocks and a red cross picked up the wounded student when the CRS were around the photographer. When the CRS saw them they threw an offensive grenade at them. One of the attendants, a young girl, was hit in the leg by fragments from the grenade (IA 117).

Testimony 467 (given by a student): The student was at the barricades on the 24th of May and was wounded by a grenade fragment. The student was picked up in a private car by a medical doctor. Soon they were stopped by CRS and beaten with nightsticks. They were taken to the police station in the fifth arrondissement and later to Beaujon, where police hit him on his wound with a club. The student was kept there before being taken to Marmottan Hospital (IA 18).

Testimony 785 (given by a student and first aid attendant): On the night of 24-25 May two students, one of which was a medical student, were driving in the Rue des Irlandais when, suddenly, they found themselves in front of a demolished barricade with a lot of CRS, or mobile police, in the area. They came out of the carriage doors of a building into the street. When they saw the car, they ran towards it and started yelling insults like mad dogs, accusing the occupants of giving help and information to the "insurgents" [*sic*]. They wanted to get the occupants out of the car and make them stand in front of them as they charged down the street. The two students refused to get out of the car, so the police ripped off the green crosses on the car and pummeled it with the butts of their rifles. The driver was struck on his left arm. After that, the driver backed up as fast as he could to get away. The students then drove to the big barricade at Denfert Square. There were other Red Cross ambulances there, too. Before attacking the barricade, police shot grenades in their direction to force them to back up. Police took the demonstrators they caught into the park, where they were left, after beating them up with their nightsticks. Some managed to get to the ambulances, while others remained motionless on the ground (IA 118).

Testimony 397 (given by a first aid attendant): A nurse wearing a white smock was inside a private vehicle used as a service ambulance, with the typical signs such as blue crosses. The ambulance was stopped by the police and searched. The passengers were frisked and the blue cross was ripped off the car. The attendant's white smock was torn by the police. Photographs were taken but the photographer was assaulted, the camera was broken and the film (12 photos of Beaumarchais Boulevard) was taken away. They were ordered to leave the area, after which three teargas canisters were thrown into the trunk of their car. A motorcycle policeman gave them a fire extinguisher to put out the canisters. A lieutenant of the gendarmerie based at Sarreguemines in the Moselle said, "Sir, what the CRS is doing is scandalous. I dissociate myself as a human being from what they are doing" (IA 119).

Testimony 788: A car used as an ambulance equipped with a flag and blue cross was stopped on Saint-Michel Boulevard on the night of 24-25 May. An occupant of the vehicle was holding a young girl who was injured. She was being taken to a first aid center when the police attacked. The windows of the car were broken, the girl was thrown outside on the ground and beaten; the driver of the ambulance was beaten, too, resulting in several wounds including cranial trauma. On June 11th the witness saw a student hit in the head with a grenade at Sorbonne Square at 6:40 a.m. Students went inside the Sorbonne for protection, but they were surrounded and beaten by police, and dragged to a van by their hair. Police tore people's clothing and began strangling the first aid worker with the straps of his smock. They also tore up his first aid papers. Inside the police van they were punched and slapped and insulted and hit on a wound to make it bleed. At the police station in Panthéon Square in the fifth arrondissement, they were beaten before being taken to Beaujon (IA 120).

Numerous medical personnel, doctors and first aid attendants, were arrested in May, preventing injured persons from receiving the medical attention they needed. At the precinct station in the seventh arrondissement there were about ten first aid attendants, about ten medical students, a certified nurse, and two interns from a Paris hospital in custody (IA 120).

Testimony 517: Ten first aid attendants were arrested and held in custody at the Invalides-Grenelle Station in the seventh arrondissement on 24-25 May, despite the fact that they had shown their medical identification cards. Needless to say it was a serious obstacle to the performance of their profession (IA 121).

In France, as in most countries, it is a crime not to give assistance to a person in danger, under Article 223-6 of the Penal Code. But the persons that recorded the numerous testimonies could not find a legal definition for the behavior of the police because it was so unusual. It involved the obstruction of assistance to injured persons: preventing medical personnel from gaining access to the places where injured persons could be found; impeding the circulation of service ambulances; arresting first aid workers and even doctors; attacking, intimidating or even beating first aid workers; destroying or stealing first aid material; and seizing injured persons already under the care of medical attendants (IA 122). Prolonging the suffering of injured persons or aggravating that suffering is simply antithetical to the basic moral values cherished by most in a civilized society. Yet the testimonies against the police and CRS are damning, to say the least.

Testimony 532: Witnesses saw what happened from their apartment window, Rue Monsieur-le-Prince, on Saturday, 25 May between 4:30-5:30 a.m., after the police had dispersed the demonstrators. A CRS van, license plate number 7997FP78, blocked the street at the cross street of Saint-Michel Boulevard. France-Inter radio had announced that the

Latin Quarter was no longer congested and that it was possible to drive through it.

Ten CRS brought all the young people that passed through there and forced them to lean against the police van. Then the CRS began beating them all at the same time with their clubs and rifle butts, or they kicked them. They hit them in the head, in the stomach or below the stomach, and pushed their heads against the car until they could no longer stand up. After beating them they checked their identity. Some were let go, others were put in the van. Some were still beaten in the van.

Testimony 386: On Saturday, 25 May at the intersection of Pleyel, a police car stopped and the officers got out and hit a tall young man carrying a poster in the head. He did not defend himself. The police savagely hit him in the head and the entire body, and continued to beat him when he was on the ground. They dragged him into the police van and continued to beat him up as he cried out (IA 139).

Testimony 414: A student was driving home on Saturday, May 25th at about 2:30 a.m. Since all the bridges were blocked by the CRS, he had to take a detour by way of the city center. He was stopped by the CRS who searched his car. They found a crank arm that he used to change a flat tire. This had been declared an offensive weapon, though virtually all cars were equipped with one because you cannot change a tire without it. He was taken to the police station. He was not questioned, but one of the policemen said to take "the son-of-a-bitch" in. He was kicked and clubbed on the feet. When he was hit on the feet he was asked if it hurt. Fortunately he did not say anything, because those that did were hit even harder. Before he was pushed into a van he was beaten with billy clubs. He was wearing a suit and a tie at the time. After that he was "more or less respected," though that was not the case with other youths who were beaten up, clubbed, punched, hit with elbows, kicked, and thrust against the side of a car to purposely make them hit their heads (IA 140).

What did the police say when they were doing these things? Things like, "So, you call us SS, ok, we're going to show you how the SS behave, you bastards," or "You've got a police record now. You're screwed," or "You bunch of stupid jerks, you killed two of ours, we're going to get even," or "We'll do the same thing to you we did to the Arabs. We killed 150 of them. You didn't know that, did you?" or "We should throw them in the Seine, but that would dirty the Seine," or "You're the one that killed our buddy, and who shot him in the balls, you bastards" (IA 141).

Those who were taken away in the police vans were first beaten up inside the vehicles by the police who arrested them, or by others. When the van arrived at the station, the cops in the vehicle reminded their colleagues to be sure to get even (IA 141).

Testimony 506: Report given for 23-24 May at 2:15 a.m. by a student. The racism of the police was all too obvious. A young Englishman was thoroughly beaten up and a young Arab "polarized their attention." He was insulted and severely beaten all the way to the station. One of the cops hit him in the face with his rifle butt; as a result his face was all bloody and swollen. Cops took pleasure in hitting people on their joints (sensitive parts of the body).

Testimony 481: One of the goals of the police was to terrorize the arrestees, telling them they would be hanged or thrown into the Seine (*which calls to mind Gilles Tautin*), or beaten up and left in a field somewhere.

It should be noted that most of the persons arrested were

young, 16 to 25 for the most part, and had no experience with institutionalized brutality.

Testimony 388: During the night of 25-26 May this person was pasting messages on a billboard at the Pleyel intersection when he was surprised by a police patrol. He tried briefly to escape without success, and let himself be apprehended without resistance. At that point, the police surrounded him and violently beat him, throwing him down on the sidewalk, and beating him as they put him into the van. The police beat him up all the way to the station in Saint-Denis, where he remained from 12:30 a.m. to 3:00 a.m., and forced him to keep his hands on his head because he was threatened and brutalized. A lieutenant decided to take him for a ride in a Peugeot with three other agents for an unknown destination. The car stopped in a back street of an isolated area, and he had to get out, whereupon he was beaten again. At that point he managed to escape by cutting across a field and arrived in a nearby village where he asked for directions.

At the station, apart from other death threats, the police would say, "Monday we'll shoot the demonstrators. We really hope you'll shoot at one of us so that we're free to do what we want." When the police saw his papers, they took him for a foreigner, a Jew. The police threatened him twice, saying they would throw him in the Seine (IA 144).

Testimony 622: This witness evokes the "welcoming committee" that many other witnesses mentioned. After being arrested at 5 a.m. by a CRS blockade on the Sully Bridge, along with the couple that picked them up in their car, they were taken to the police station in the fourth arrondissement. There was blood on the tile floor and the sound of cries in the background. After verification of their identity, a door was opened to a hallway ten meters long, where the

CRS and mobile police were lined up, shoulder to shoulder. The arrestees were kicked and slapped as they walked by; women were felt up. After the "welcoming committee" they were placed in a small cell with fifty people crammed in it. The air was suffocating (IA 145).

Testimony 407: When the arrestees arrived at the station, they were met inside by a "welcoming committee": two rows of CRS who kicked people as they went by. After that they passed into a corridor where they were punched and kicked.

Testimony 385: This report was given by a young woman instructor. At the time of the arrest, although she did not try to resist and obeyed orders, she was hit several times with a billy club on the foot and fist. Upon arriving at the precinct station, she was hit with a nightstick on the thighs. When she entered the station, she was punched in the face and kicked and insulted. The CRS threatened to rape her and suggested taking off her clothes. She was the only girl inside the station at the time. The guy that kicked and punched her was named "Jules." The young woman also saw a CRS officer take bolts out of his own pocket and then claim to have taken them out of the pocket of the boy next to her. Several CRS beat up the youth because of that lie (IA 153).

In the police van youths were kicked and punched all the way to the station. Inside the station arrestees were grouped together and beaten. Twice, youths were taken out of the cell when they had just been put in and "beaten again for good measure," the CRS said. Some cops got drunk on wine after a high ranking officer left. He was called "the prefect," so it must have been Maurice Grimaud (IA 154). *This testimony supposes then that the prefect, Maurice Grimaud, was aware of the inhuman, barbaric treatment inside the stations, as well as the conditions of detention.*

Testimony 408: All night long young people arrived at

the station on 24-25 May. The student said some gave out terrifying screams when they were beaten in the station, Rue François-Miron in the fourth arrondissement. One cop hit people with both fists when they arrived, and did this while they were being held by other cops. They were violently kicked when they were on the ground. After which they were lifted up by the police only to be thrust head-first against the cell door, yelling as they did so, "Watch out, it's not open!" Outside the cell the cops would say, "It would be funny to lob a few teargas grenades in there," or "We should throw gasoline on them and burn them all" (IA 158).

When they were being put back in the vans, a cop gave the order to shoot them if anyone tried to get away. Many of the remarks made by the police and CRS were sexual in nature, as were the gestures of caressing and fondling, and were punctuated by laughs of satisfaction.

Blacks and North Africans were mistreated more than others because of their race and color (*Testimony 416*, IA 169).

Testimony 502: Parents were not told exactly when their sons and daughters would be freed. A CRS commander went before a crowd of parents outside Beaujon, Rue de Courcelles, and started giving a lesson in morality [*sic*], saying that the next time police would start shooting.

Once freed, there was the danger of the youths being arrested again, because there were police and CRS roaming the streets everywhere. Beaujon could have given a certificate of safe conduct to the persons released, but they didn't. Some of the youths had been so severely beaten they had trouble walking and had to be helped. The expression on their faces was proof they had been terrorized, that their human dignity had been despoiled (IA 179).

Flins is a small village in the Yvelines, about fourteen

kilometers from Mantes-la-Jolie. It is well-known for its Renault automobile factory. On 16 May 1968, a strike began in Flins at 2 p.m., and the factory was occupied. A red revolutionary flag was hoisted. The strike continued for three weeks.

During the night of 5-6 June (Wednesday and Thursday) the CRS invaded the factory and threw the striking pickets out. About 1,000 CRS, gendarmes and mobile police surrounded the factory at three in the morning. Those occupying the factory left without major incidents.

Students arrived on Thursday, 6 June. In an effort to isolate the factory, police stopped all cars coming from Paris at the entrance to the motorway; the vehicles were searched and the occupants frisked before being taken to Beaujon. When they were released, they found the tires of their cars systematically slashed (IA 181).

At the end of a meeting at the Mureaux, a small village, at about eight in the morning, police charged the crowd and chased students and workers in the village. As usual, grenades were used and ambulances were prevented from doing their job.

On Monday, 10 June at about four in the afternoon, twenty university students, high school students and workers were discussing strategy in an isolated spot on the bank of an island in the Seine, near the Meulan bridge. According to the testimony of Jean T, the group was surprised by gendarmes that had surrounded them, charging with their rifle butts forward, and shouting at the group to jump in the water: "In the drink! In the drink!" (IA 184). Those who could jumped in the river, those that couldn't were beaten with rifle butts. A comrade was pushed into the Seine River after being hit with a rifle butt. They saw Gilles Tautin sink in the water. "Stop, somebody's drowning!" they yelled. No assistance was given because police were too busy arresting people. A gendarme hit somebody with his billy club as he was getting out of the water. The mayor of Mureaux got his badge number, so it would be possible to identify the officer.

The prefecture of the Yvelines issued a communiqué in the evening of the tragedy, and its version of the drowning is diametrically opposed to the students' version. The prefecture supported the gendarmes by saying Gilles Tautin voluntarily jumped in the water to get away from the gendarmes. The forensic doctors Martin and Lecœur stated there were no marks of physical violence on the body. One must admit that it is a little hard to believe that someone would voluntarily jump into a river with a strong current.

Whether they were students taken from the blazing barricades, curious onlookers, local residents trying to get home, a fly poster far from the billy clubs and the teargas, a medical doctor, or a first aid attendant attempting to assist persons in danger, those who were apprehended were victims of physical abuse, insults, threats and humiliation in the police vehicles, when getting out of them, or inside the police stations where no one else could see what was happening. People are supposed to be innocent until proven guilty, but the testimonies show many were systematically deprived of their constitutional rights.

A strange, sadistic ritual occurred during the months of May and June in which those not wearing uniforms were the "offenders," the "enemy," the "insurgents" that must be forced to submit. After taking the rounds of the precinct stations, the prisoners ended up at Beaujon. Quite a few mistreated people would spend more than twenty-four hours there and claim afterwards that they had had a nightmarish experience in the detention center.

The documented testimonies gathered by UNEF and

SNE-sup are damning and proof that Christian Fouchet and Maurice Grimaud's police repeatedly and knowingly violated French law. "The action there was collective" (IA 137). Those same testimonies provide evidence that the abuse of authority had nothing to do with restoring law and order. For the most part, it was gratuitous. "Abandon all hope ye who enter here," seemed to be the unwritten code at the precinct stations. Simply being there, for whatever reason, seemed to justify being brutalized.

The persons detained in the police stations and at Beaujon did not, while they were in custody, constitute a threat to society or the police. So what was the purpose of the sadistic acts? Were they symptoms of deeper, more serious ills such as xenophobia, racism, sexism and the pathological need to subjugate and inflict pain? How was it that high-ranking officials who boasted of the nation's democratic institutions could close their eyes to vile practices associated with despotic, dictatorial regimes based on moral depravity?

The Consequences of May 68

After the May crisis, de Gaulle changed his Prime Minister Georges Pompidou, naming Maurice Couve de Murville to the post. He was more discreet than Pompidou and probably lacked his charisma. Pompidou left Matignon with a feeling of bitterness that he kept well-hidden. In a conversation with his adviser Jacques Foccart, on 13 October 1967, de Gaulle had expressed his desire of dissolving the National Assembly and reportedly said, "Pompidou, now, is finished. I'm going to name somebody else to the post. I can't go on like this. He's not implementing my policies, and always fiddling, fixing things up. But he's not there to fix things up. But you see, he hasn't got any balls." Foccart persuaded him to leave well enough alone, for the time being anyway.

Officially, Pompidou was being kept "in reserve for the Republic." Was de Gaulle afraid of something? Maybe he didn't want to see his prime minister becoming too important, too soon. Of course the Gaullists and Georges Pompidou were the big winners in the legislative elections in June.

The constitutional referendum held on 27 April 1969, would have changed the Senate and decentralized the government. It goes without saying that the political opposition wanted to see the General resign, so they told people to vote "no." To complicate things, Pompidou had declared himself candidate for the presidency. Moreover, there was discord among friends.

At the time, most citizens were probably not opposed to creating administrative regions, which in fact were created later, nor were they strongly opposed to changing the Senate. In truth, the vote soon became focused on the president: keeping de Gaulle or not. François Mauriac called the referendum political suicide, which in a sense is what it turned out to be, like a game of Russian roulette. People voted "no" on the referendum, and Charles de Gaulle resigned the next day. But the election was a lot closer than the percentages appeared to show, with 53.2% voting against the changes. According to Pierre Messmer, Charles de Gaulle left the Élysée on the evening of the referendum, so he was prepared ahead of time for the defeat.

Political analysts have often asked themselves why the French voted "no" on the referendum. There are probably several reasons. The Gaullists had begun their campaign later than the opposition, so they had to catch up. Georges Pompidou, former Prime Minister, declared his candidacy while in Rome on 17 January 1969. Many voters probably believed that de Gaulle and Pompidou had made the decision together, although that was not the case. Valéry Giscard d'Estaing publicly said he would vote "no," and members of the UDR did not hesitate to reject the referendum. In the polls, the "yes" vote, which initially had 60%, began to disintegrate. Charles de Gaulle had said he would leave office when he was eighty years old. At the time of the referendum he was seventy-eight.

May 68 was largely about the conflict of generations: youth versus the older generation, the generation that had fought World War Two. But the young people that defended the barricades in the streets of Paris were not the flower children of the Haight-Ashbury, though quite a few knew something about *les paradis artificiels*.

The flower power movement in San Francisco was not politically militant, even if Timothy Leary, advocate of psychedelic drugs, scared the pants off conservatives like Richard Nixon because of his ability to influence American youth. Flower children did not dig up the streets, overturn cars, build barricades, or throw cobblestones. May 68 involved several politically militant groups that wanted to start a revolution, at least that is what many said publicly. That might explain some of the brutality of the CRS, though not all of it. In any event, May 68 was about creating political, social and economic change. The change did take place, although a lot of it was adulterated.

Part of the social change that was asked for concerned sexual mores. The 22 March Movement criticized the dormitory system at the University of Nanterre because it separated the sexes. The Movement also denounced sexual stereotypes as a means of perpetuating a corrupt and sexist society.

The counterculture of the sixties was all for sexual liberation. Sex was not something dirty or something to be ashamed of, it was a natural human function that helped people to be happy and healthy. The sexual revolution, explored by the psychedelic counterculture of the Haight-Ashbury, was linked to the larger revolution against the bourgeois, capitalist system which alienated people and kept them from achieving their full potential.

Part of the liberation was related to birth control. Running the risk of becoming pregnant when one was not married was a serious problem that young women had to deal with. On 28 December 1967, the Law Neuwirth in France authorized the sale of contraceptives, but the law was not put into practice until 1972. The birth control pill was authorized for sale by the Federal Drug Administration in the United States in 1960.

To some extent, May 68 helped to spawn the feminist

movement in France. The Women's Liberation Movement (MLF) criticized the patriarchal society because it was responsible, it felt, for many of society's social ills, including war and exploitation. The French movement was influenced by Women's Lib in the United States. Women such as Monique Wittig, Antoinette Fouque, Josiane Chanel and others were meeting with other women in 1968 to discuss women's rights and the role of women in society. The first meeting of the MLF was officially held at the University of Vincennes in the spring of 1970, and their first publicized media event was on 26 August 1970, when a group of women placed a bouquet of flowers at the Arc de Triomphe in Paris for the wife of the Unknown Soldier.

May 68 began in an institution of higher learning. Students in Nanterre and elsewhere knew the educational system desperately needed to be reformed. The reform that followed was a result of the events in May 68. Generally speaking, teaching became more flexible and secondary schools became les autocratic. The student-teacher relationship changed as personal attitudes changed. Before 1968 teaching was often based on fear and punishment, but after the May revolt, students became active participants in the teaching process. Pedagogical techniques and objectives changed as a result, with an attempt at developing autonomy and more interaction. Respect was no longer a one way street, teachers also had a professional and moral obligation to show respect towards their pupils. Parents and pupils were also permitted to attend class councils after May 1968.

Edgar Faure became Minister of Education, and the law named after him was passed on 12 November 1968. This testifies to the government's desire to reform quickly. The law changed the administrative structure of universities, making them more autonomous. The different schools and colleges of the universities were changed into teaching and research units (UER), and university councils were created in which students, university technicians, administrative employees and persons outside the university could become members. The goal, whether achieved or not, was to create transparency and openness, though it is doubtful it really improved things for teachers or students. Another important aspect of the reform was the desire to achieve multidisciplinarity by combining the broad domains of research and teaching: professors were expected to do both, of course.

Georges Pompidou probably was elected president because the referendum was rejected and because of May 68. This seems clear in light of the legislative landslide in favor of the Gaullists on 23 and 30 June 1968. Pompidou represented modernity, while de Gaulle epitomized the past, though he realized that the country's public and private institutions needed to be modernized. France had great ambitions, and Pompidou was there to make its dreams come true, to attempt to equal German industry and perhaps become as egalitarian as Sweden at the same time. So the new president set about developing French industry, investing in high-speed trains like the TGV, modernizing telecommunications, constructing motorways, developing a satellite launcher, and more.

If the Gaullists were favored by the May revolt, communist regimes were denounced as totalitarian and imperialistic. As a result, leftists lost representatives in the National Assembly.

Workers gained from the strikes and demonstrations of May and June. Before May 1968, employees worked long hours, sometimes fifty or more a week for low pay. After May salaries were increased by 10% and the minimum wage by about 35%. The work week was reduced to forty hours with a maximum of forty-eight hours per week. Union groups were established within companies, along with union delegates in enterprises of fifty employees or more. In addition, there was pay for striking hours.

The Glorious Thirty would continue for a few more years, but Georges Pompidou's vast program of modernization would be slowed down by the first petroleum crisis of 1973.

Conclusion

May 68 was a crisis of many sorts that illustrated some of the inadequacies of civilization. It was the most important social movement in France in the twentieth century, but nobody could say they had expected it. It seemed to materialize out of thin air, beginning on an obscure university campus in the Paris suburbs and spreading like wildfire to the capital, the provinces, the workplace, Matignon, and the Élysée Palace. Soon the byword of the sixties was echoed by radicals and the media: Revolution. But could a revolution occur during a time of economic prosperity? And who would be willing to play for high stakes when the going got tough?

Youth tries to make up for its lack of experience with enthusiasm, and so it was with the May movement in France. But radical students got lost somewhere in their dreams of supplanting the Gaullists with the questionable help of the CFDT, while at the same time keeping the PCF at bay. However you want to look at it, the idea of fomenting a revolution was a Marxist pipedream.

The euphoric meeting at Charléty would be a key to their success or failure. The CGT, the most influential and powerful union in France, did not want to start a *real* revolution. That was for the scruffy longhairs of the UJCML, 22 March, JCR or FER to take care of. Georges Séguy was a man of experience who had worked for the French Resistance and been arrested by the Nazi Gestapo. He knew how power functions and how it corrupts. Discreetly, the CGT would put a leash on the exuberant student movement and take it for a walk in the park. Séguy knew a good thing when he saw it, too, and accepted the Grenelle Protocol, which was an important step forward for unions and workers, even though it was rejected in the beginning by the rank and file.

"Everything is possible" was a key slogan from Charléty. When you believe you are the vanguard of a revolution you have to dream, and French youth were dreaming of change in all aspects of life. "It's a sad thing not to have friends, but it's even sadder not to have enemies," said Che Guevara. The youth movement did not have any trouble making enemies, but it had more of those than it did friends.

Could the government survive? It was seriously questioned by the non-confidence vote in the assembly. Although that was rejected, the main issues facing de Gaulle and Pompidou were not resolved. Leftists were hoping the Fifth Republic–established by de Gaulle on 4 October 1958–would fold, though it was just catching its breath. How could an erratic, emotional student movement triumph over the well-established forces of Gaullism and communism? The radical left had neither the resources nor the organizational capability to pull it off. "You can improvise a riot, but not a revolution," remarked Adrien Dansette. Distributing political tracts, occupying buildings, making barricades and throwing Molotov cocktails may be fun, but you have to see into the future and devise a workable strategy on how to get there. That is if you really want to slay a Leviathan.

The abortive attempt at revolution did accomplish certain things, but was there a revolution in French universities? Well, perhaps a kind of revolution that gave students more power–the kind of power that could be used against students, professors or administrators by those who happened to be in control at the time.

As is often the case when different groups are grabbing

for power, the various factions within the student movement, which consisted of a very small minority of all the students, were pushing and shoving to get up the ladder before their rivals did. Those groups were the Trotskyites, Maoists, Marxists, Leninists, situationists, antifascists, *et al.*

One area in which radicals were blatantly ignorant involved the mechanisms of an industrialized consumer society. Jean-Marie Domenach, a leftwing writer and intellectual, noted that "One had never seen revolutionaries so lacking in theories." Theory was replaced by impassioned pleas for rebellion and radical change, and those involve resistance and violence. How many of the Maoists knew that Chairman Mao was probably the greatest mass murderer of all time?

Daniel Cohn-Bendit, the Asterix of the agitators, had an answer for everything: "The most important thing is not to devise reform for capitalist society, but to create an experience that clashes completely with that society, an experience that does not last. You see a fleeting image and then it is suddenly gone. But that's enough to prove that it can exist."

When experiences are over they are soon forgotten, and when images disappear, they cease to exist for most people. The May student movement was confined to an extremely small group of radicals, so the base was too narrow to support a vast movement.

Some spoke of foreign involvement, but it was limited and superficial. The same thing was said of the antiwar movement in the United States. But most protestors there were not ideological Marxists, and you did not have to be a Marxist to know that American imperialism in Southeast Asia was morally wrong and, in the long run, not in the interests of the United States.

By the same token, you did not have to be a Maoist or a

Trotskyist to know that a large percentage of the population in France was not sharing in the prosperity but was being exploited, or that the national slogan–Liberty, Equality, Fraternity–had little meaning for those at the bottom of the social-economic pyramid.

The French revolt was made in France. The Mad Dogs and the rest of the "trouble makers" revolted against a certain kind of society that placed material values before human values. The model for that certain kind of society, however, was made in the United States of America.

Was the French revolt a "psychodrama" as Raymond Aron said. It is possible to see it that way, but it went deeper than that. May 68 involved a rejection of the values of the establishment, and that revolt had become international, transcending borders and language barriers. It was a human revolt against dehumanization. "Gilles Tautin took my place," said Alain Geismar (BAY 242). Victim of violence, Gilles Tautin served perhaps as a kind of scapegoat so that some sort of atonement could be achieved. His death marked the end of the Movement and "the end of the Leninist mythology of the revolution." The "revolutionaries" of May 68 were not prepared to die for the cause. They were not prepared to go all the way.

Acronyms

CAL   High School Action Committees (Comités d'action lycéens)

CFDT French Democratic Confederation of Labor (Confédération française démocratique du travail)

CFTC French Confederation of Christian Workers (Fédération française des travailleurs chrétiens)

CGC   French Confederation of Management (Confédération générale des cadres)

CGT   General Confederation of Labor (Confédération générale du travail)

CNPF National Council of French Employers (Conseil national du patronat français)

CRS   Republican Security Companies (Compagnies républicaines de sécurité)

DST   Directorate of Territorial Surveillance (Direction de la Surveillance du territoire)

EDF   Electricity of France (Électricité de France)

FEN   Federation of National Education (Fédération de l'Éducation nationale)

FER   Federation of Revolutionary Students (Fédération des étudiants révolutionnaires)

FGDS   Federation of the Democratic and Socialist Left (Fédération de la gauche démocrate et socialiste)

JCR   Communist Revolutionary Youth (Jeunesse communiste révolutionnaire)

MAU   University Action Movement (Mouvement d'action universitaire)

CVN   National Vietnam Committee (Comité Vietnam national)

OAS   Secret Army Organisation (Organisation armée secrète)

ORTF   Office of French Radio and Television Diffusion (Office de radiodiffusion-télévision française)

PCF   French Communist Party (Parti communiste français)

PSU   Unified Socialist Party (Parti socialiste unifié)

SDS   Socialist German Student Union (Sozialistisher Deutscher Studentenbund)

SMIG   minimum guaranteed interprofessional salary (salaire minimum interprofessionnel garanti)

SNE-sup National Union of Higher Education (Syndicat national de l'enseignement supérieur)

SNCF   National Society of French Railways (Société natio-
        nale des chemins de fer français)

UJCML Union of Communist Youth Marxist-Leninist (Un-
        ion des jeunesses communistes marxistes-léninistes)

UNEF   National Union of Students of France (Union natio-
        nale des étudiants de France)

Bibliography & Abbreviations

(BAY)   Baynac, Jacques. *Mai retrouvé*. Paris: 1978.

(BER)   Bertolino, Jean. *Les Troublions*. Paris: Stock, 1969.

(BUR)   Burlet, Laurent. "Mai 68: mystères autour de la mort du commissaire Lacroix," 1 May 2008.
         <http://www.lyoncapitale.fr/Journal/Lyon/Culture/Histoir
         e/Mai-68-mysteres-autour-de-la-mort-du-commissaire-
         Lacroix>

(CHA)   Chabrun, Laurent, Jérôme Dupuis and Jean-Marie Pon-
         taut, "Mai 68: Les archives secrètes de la police," 19
         March 1998.
         <https://www.lexpress.fr/informations/mai-68-les-
         archives-secretes-de-la-police_628297.html>

(COH)   Cohn-Bendit, Daniel. *Le Grand Bazar*. Paris: Belfond,
         1975.

(DAN)   Dansette, Adrien. *Mai 1968*. Paris: Plon, 1971.

(DRE)   Dreyfus-Armand, Geneviève et Daniel Cohn-Bendit. "Le
         mouvement du 22 mars." Entretien avec Daniel Cohn-
         Bendit. *Matériaux pour l'histoire de notre temps*, n° 11-
         13, 1988. *Mai-68. Les mouvements étudiants en France et
         dans le monde.*

(DUT)   Interview with Jean-Pierre Duteuil for Radio Libertaire,
         "Le mouvement du 22 mars," May 1988.
         <http://increvablesanarchistes.org/articles/1968/68_22mar
         s.htm>

(FAU)   Fauré, Christine. *Mai 68. Jour et nuit*. Paris: Découvertes Gallimard, 1998.

(GRI)   Grimaud, Maurice. *En mai fais ce qu'il te plaît*. Paris: Stock, 1977.

(HAM)   Hamon, Hervé and Patrick Rotman. *Génération. Les Années de rêve*. Paris: Seuil, 1987.

(JOF)   Joffrin, Laurent *Mai 68. Histoire des événements*. Paris: Seuil, 1988.

(KER)   Kerbourc'h, Jean-Claude. *Le Piéton de mai*. Paris: Julliard, 1968.

(LAC)   Lacouture, Jean. *De Gaulle*, tome III, *Le Souverain*. Paris: Seuil, 1986.

(GOF)   Le Goff, Jean-Pierre. *Mai 68. L'héritage impossible*. Paris: La Découverte, 1998.

(MAG)   Magneron, Jean-Luc. *Mai 68. La belle ouvrage*. DVD, Warner Vision France, 60 minutes.

(ROU)   Roussel, Éric. *Pompidou*. Paris: Lattès, 1984.

(SEG)   Séguy, Georges. *Le Mai de la C.G.T.* Paris : Julliard, 1972.

(SIR)   Sirinelli, Jean-François *Mai 68*. Paris: Biblis, May 2013.

(IA)   UNEF, SNE-sup. *Ils accusent*. Paris: Seuil, 1968.

(LN)   UNEF, SNE-sup. *Le Livre noir des journées de Mai*. Paris: Seuil, 1968.

Index

F

Faure, Edgar, 139
Ferlinghetti, Lawrence, 68
Foccart, Jacques, 77, 104, 135
Fouchet, Christian, 31, 54, 57,
    58, 75, 77, 78, 81, 82, 84, 99,
    134
Fouque, Antoinette, 138
Frachon, Benoît, 91

G

Gauban, Daniel, 91
Geismar, Alain, 38, 42, 43, 46,
    52, 58, 61, 63, 81, 82, 83, 94,
    96
Ginsberg, Allen, 67
Gonin, Marcel, 97
Grappin, Pierre, 15, 17, 20
Grimaud, Maurice, 3, 22, 27,
    28, 30, 31, 32, 39, 42, 43, 44,
    54, 58, 59, 60, 69, 75, 77, 78,
    81, 82, 83, 85, 93, 99, 130,
    134, 150

H

Halbeher, Aimé, 94
Hayden, Tom, 12
Hébert, Alexandre, 72
Heurgon, Marc, 96
Ho Chi Minh, 9
Honorin, Michel, 77
Hutin, Jean-Pierre, 77
Huvelin, Paul, 80, 91

J

Jankelevitch, Vladimir, 10
Jeanneney, Jean-Marcel, 91, 94
Jobert, Michel, 75
Johnson, Lyndon, 10
Joxe, Louis, 31, 32, 57, 58
Juquin, Pierre, 21

K

Kahn, Marcel-Francis, 96
Kastler, Alfred, 10, 42
Kennedy, John F., 9
Kennedy, Robert, 13
Kervendaël, Yves, 22
King, Martin Luther, 11, 13
Krasucki, Henri, 91
Krieg, Pierre-Charles, 100

L

Langlade, Xavier, 15
Lebel, Jean-Jacques, 67
Lefebvre, Henri, 34
Louet, Roger, 92

M

Ma Van Lau, 49
Maire, Jean, 91
Malcom X, 11
Malterre, André, 92
Marangé, James, 38, 57, 92
Marcellin, Raymond, 23
Marchais, Georges, 21, 33, 63
Massu, Jacques, 102, 103
Matherion, Philippe, 88

W

Weber, Henri, 25
Wittig, Monique, 138

Z

Zamansky, Marc, 42

ABOUT THE AUTHOR

William Schnabel was born in Sacramento, California, in 1949 and grew up in the San Francisco Bay Area. During the 1960s he was an eyewitness and participant in a number of events involving the civil rights movement, demonstrations against the Vietnam War, the free speech movement, and protests by the Black Panthers and Students for a Democratic Society. He lived for a time in the Haight-Ashbury in the sixties and attended many of the dance concerts at the local ballrooms.

He graduated from U. C. Berkeley and took courses at San Francisco State before moving to France where he lives today. As a university professor there, he edited *Les Cahiers du GERF* in Grenoble, and taught courses in American history, culture and literature, and specialized classes on the sixties and science fiction. He has published numerous articles and books on the 1960s, science fiction, and on American culture and literature. His latest books include *Summer of Love and Haight* and *George Orwell's 1984.*

Printed in Great Britain
by Amazon